Racial Harmony Is Achievable

Racial and social relations can become harmonious and serene in every country of the world. Racism can be eliminated. The Kingdom of Hawai'i during the nineteenth century reveals a history of responsive politicians, economic progress, environmental preservation, and serene race relations because of a cultural lifestyle that can be emulated. But not everything was rosy. Severe challenges emerged after the discovery of the Islands in 1778. The leaders and the people responded to various intrusions in an exemplary manner, while the same problems have provoked endless conflict and social disintegration that plague the world today.

Using analytical methods, this book recounts how the people of the Islands overcame civil wars, decimating diseases, ecosystem despoliation, religious conflicts, the uprooting of feudalism, worker exploitation, imperialist threats, coups, and a massive influx of new residents who quickly became acculturated. But the Kingdom of Hawai'i ended because of a flagrant violation of international law that calls out to be reversed.

The world needs to know how a society of Caucasians, Chinese, Japanese, Mexicans, Native Hawaiians, and others worked together to solve problems that seem intractable elsewhere. Until the secret is revealed, the world seems doomed to constant turbulence. Presenting a plan for social transformation, this book will be of key interest in the fields of political science, public affairs, sociology, and Hawaiian studies.

Michael Haas is an Emeritus Professor of Political Science at the University of Hawai'i, USA. He has also held many visiting positions at a number of USA- and UK-based universities. The author of more than fifty books, he was nominated for a Nobel Peace Prize in 2009.

Racial Harmony Is Achievable

Lessons from the Kingdom of Hawai'i

Michael Haas

Routledge
Taylor & Francis Group

LONDON AND NEW YORK

First published 2017
by Routledge
2 Park Square, Milton Park, Abingdon, Oxon OX14 4RN

and by Routledge
605 Third Avenue, New York, NY 10017

First issued in paperback 2021

Routledge is an imprint of the Taylor & Francis Group, an informa business

Publisher's Note
The publisher has gone to great lengths to ensure the quality of
this reprint but points out that some imperfections in the
original copies may be apparent.

British Library Cataloguing in Publication Data
A catalogue record for this book is available from the British Library

Library of Congress Cataloging-in-Publication Data
A catalog record for this book has been requested

ISBN 13: 978-1-03-209780-0 (pbk)
ISBN 13: 978-1-138-20446-1 (hbk)

Typeset in Times New Roman
by Apex CoVantage, LLC

Contents

Tables

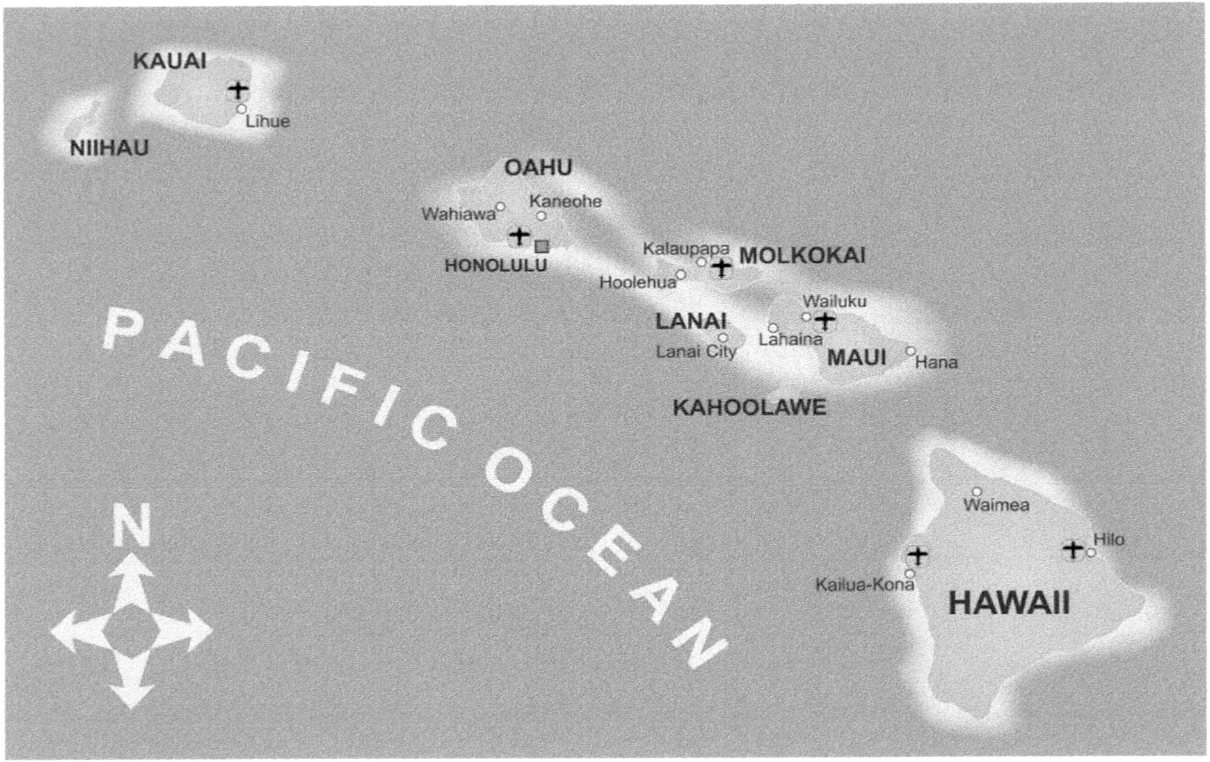
KAUAI
Lihue
NIIHAU
OAHU
Wahiawa
Kaneohe
HONOLULU
Kalaupapa
MOLKOKAI
Hoolehua
Wailuku
LANAI
Lahaina
Lanai City
MAUI
Hana
KAHOOLAWE
PACIFIC OCEAN
N
Waimea
Hilo
Kailua-Kona
HAWAII

Preface

In 1964, as I was finishing my doctoral dissertation at Stanford University, I received a job offer for a one-year appointment as Assistant Professor of Political Science at the University of Hawaiʻi's main campus in Mānoa Valley, Honolulu. I accepted, though I never had visited the Islands before and knew nobody there. The only person whom I was told to look up was Bishop Museum curator Kenneth Emory, father-in-law of my godmother in Detroit.

Not long after arriving to take up my appointment, I realized that the businesslike environment among faculty, mostly from the continental United States, was entirely different from the more personable residents who were born in the Islands. Through participant observation as a gay person, I had the good fortune over the years to meet and live with many such remarkable "locals," as they are called colloquially. Whether as friends, partners, or tenants, I acquired from accounts of their lives keen insights into what was then called the Aloha Spirit, but which I later identified as Hawaiʻi's "multicultural ethos." My first Thanksgiving was with a Chinese-Hawaiian family in Kalihi, the working class neighborhood of Honolulu. My first roommate was Caucasian-Hawaiian. My first partner, a Filipino, introduced me to problems facing Filipinos and Native Hawaiians. And to redress their grievances, I eventually formed a multiethnic organization first known as Friends of Racial Equality and the Spirit of Hawaiian Aloha and later incorporated as the Foundation for Race/Sex Equality and the Spirit of Hawaiian Aloha. I also shared residence with young men of Afro-Cuban, Chinese, Filipino-Japanese, Japanese, Korean, and Navajo ancestry over the years.

Accordingly, I experienced firsthand how problems in the Islands are identified and resolved. I even became for a time the education chair of the local chapter of the National Association for the Advancement of Colored People. But my form of activism was primarily to engage in objective research about the Islands that brought unexpected facts to the fore. With my Filipino partner, who later died of an aneurysm, the book *Politics and*

Prejudice in Contemporary Hawai'i (1976) collected articles from local newspapers.

Some of my research was summarized within articles and op-eds in the Honolulu daily newspapers. But most of my publications have been in the form of conference papers, articles in academic journals, and a few books. I also did some lobbying at the state legislature, and I filed a few civil rights complaints. Much of that effort is recounted on pages of my books *Institutional Racism: The Case of Hawai'i* (1992) and *Looking for the Aloha Spirit: Promoting Ethnic Harmony* (2010).

On one occasion in 1994, I was asked by a representative of the U.S. Information Agency at an academic conference if I would be willing to give a talk about Hawai'i in Azerbaijan, then undergoing ethnic turmoil. Later, he informed me that the idea of the trip was not approved. Had I then been on a lecture circuit to talk about my experience and my research, the world would have been briefed on some of the secrets of Hawai'i's exemplary society. In any case, he gave me the idea for my edited book *Multicultural Hawai'i: The Fabric of a Multiethnic Society* (1998), which brought together several scholars who shared the vision of Hawai'i as a very special place.

When I retired and moved to Los Angeles in 1998 along with my partner, a Filipino-Japanese who later died of cancer, I did not anticipate the culture shock of moving from a place where many cultures are mutually respected. Instead, I discovered that multiethnic California is still living in a past era when American elites seized power from Mexicans, made the latter second-class citizens, and assumed that government and society should prevail and set the rules for all others. In other words, based on my experience in Hawai'i, I realized that I had moved from an anti-colonial state to one where government treats those outside the levers of power as colonial subjects. Another person went through the same experience in the mid-1960s – Ben Cayetano, the future Hawai'i governor who went away from home for college in Los Angeles (Cayetano 2009:ch2).

The election of Barack Obama in 2008 inspired me to edit what might be considered a second edition of my 1998 book – *Barack Obama, the Aloha Zen President* (2011). The aim was to demonstrate that the Honolulu-born 44th president of the United States exemplified the spirit of the Islands. The subtitle was even more explicit on that point – *How a Son of the 50th State May Revitalize America Based on 12 Multicultural Principles*. However, almost nobody in Washington was interested in why his personality would not conform to the contentious culture of the Beltway. Indeed, few outside the Islands seem interested in learning why Hawai'i has achieved such exemplary racial harmony (cf. Hitch 1992:181).

Although some academics elsewhere have been eager to learn about race relations in the Islands, the vast ignorance about Hawai'i compels me to write. Within the continental United States, I have the impression that troubled race relations are considered inevitable by many Blacks, while Whites in authority want to stay in control by denying that there is any such problem by believing that the accomplishments of the civil rights era remove the topic from their horizons. The present volume is my response to the important need to identify a pathway toward healing, both nationally and internationally.

Other scholars have sought to provide accounts of the Islands in various ways. Novelist James Michener did so in his book *Hawai'i* (1959), which I read in the months before my flight to take up my academic position at the University of Hawai'i. Another acclaimed book, *Hawai'i Pono: A Social History* (1961), was written by sociologist Lawrence H. Fuchs. Historian Gavan Daws penned *Shoal of Time: A History of the Hawaiian Islands* (1968) to provide information about developments from 1778 to 1959. Economist Thomas Hitch provides much socioeconomic context in his *Islands in Transition* (1992).

Living my life much closer to civil society, mid-level government officials, and those lacking political influence and interest than to the elites, I have tackled a much more controversial aspect of life in the Islands than Michener, Fuchs, and Daws – prejudice and racism. Indeed, while my work is academically respected, the fact remains that the most glaring hole in various acclaimed books of others is any serious effort to confront the main reason why Hawai'i stands out in the world – racial harmony. That so many scholars have cowardly avoided the subject is a major disgrace. Because I have played a role in that regard, I have decided to be courageous in tackling the issue, while others have presented fascinating narratives in which issues rather than people are central. Yet their writings lend important support to what I have to say.

My approach attempts a more analytic, if anthropological approach. Rather than trying to establish facts per se or extol the contributions of many important individuals in the history of the Islands, I seek explanations in the manner of a political scientist who has focused much of his career on the social anthropology behind institutional political operations. I began my scholarly career as a graduate student by writing an extensive term paper based on information within Yale University's Human Relations Area Files, including ethnographic accounts about the Hawaiian Islands, and I continue that approach in the present volume. My aim is to highlight challenges that Hawai'i has encountered over the years – challenges that have wrecked governments and ruined societies elsewhere around the globe – and how the people of the Islands have responded by turning challenges into opportunities to create a better society.

Without the help of many, I could not have produced the present volume. I am particularly indebted to of Kirstin Howgate of Ashgate Publishing, who urged me to offer two volumes about race in Hawai'i, the present one about the era before American rule, and a subsequent volume on the periods of Territorial rule and statehood.

For information cited, I want to take this opportunity to thank Ibrahim Aoudé (University of Hawai'i), Hayden Burgess (Institute for the Advancement of Hawaiian Affairs), Ben Cayetano (former governor), Gavan Daws (historian), Moses Kalei Nahonoapi'ilani Haia III (Native Hawaiian Legal Corporation), Anita Manning (Honey Bee Services), and George Simson (University of Hawai'i).

The world, in my opinion, should take careful note of challenges that have confronted the people of Hawai'i, how they have been mitigated and in many cases surmounted, and wherein the Islands' underlying philosophy embedded in cultural norms needs to be emulated. During an epoch when hopes of individuals and groups within the continents of the planet are frustrated and governments are trapped into repeating the mistakes of history, readers need to reflect how the world would be a better place by paying careful attention to what is presented in the present volume and spreading the concept of Aloha that keeps the peoples of the Islands in contented racial harmony.

Michael Haas

Part I

Introduction

Most scholars of race relations focus on the problems in order to suggest ways out of dilemmas with no clear ideal type model in mind. Instead, why not examine a place where race relations are serene to learn lessons for application elsewhere?

From the days of the Kingdom of Hawai'i, the Islands have long been known for exemplary race relations. Yet current discussion on race relations is not informed by that achievement, which was a result of conscious decisions during the nineteenth century in response to crises that have caused other parts of the world to implode.

Important decisions in the Islands were made because of a unique cultural environment that redefined the concept of "social contract" between rulers and ruled with profound implications for the environment, politics, and social life. Serene race relations were forged on the basis of norms that had behavioral consequences, which in turn reinforced the norms of racial serenity.

Hitherto, scholars have bypassed the birthplace of serene race relations in Hawai'i, considering the Islands to be too unique a situation to have any implications for application elsewhere. On the contrary, the present volume argues that there are lessons to be learned and a set of factors to be identified from the history of the Kingdom of Hawai'i that will assist the world in advancing racial harmony.

Accordingly, the present volume presents an untold story of the Hawaiian Islands, using analytical methods rather than reciting historical facts for their own sake. No other scholar has dared to do so because the sensitivity of the subject prompts caution. But without relating the factors underlying serene race relations, the world loses an opportunity to reflect on what can be done today to move the discussion forward. If Hawai'i could avoid virulent racism, why not the rest of the world? The present book, thus, provides a glimpse at a racial transformation almost unknown anywhere else in the world that must be known and trumpeted loudly.

Nevertheless, the Kingdom of Hawai'i no longer exists. The fall of that kingdom in the late nineteenth century illustrates how White racists undermined perhaps the most important social development of all time. Yet the tenacity of Islanders to undo every aspect of racial subordination began then and continues today. The story of how they have been reversing institutional forms of racism after Hawai'i became the fiftieth state of the United States in 1959 is the subject of a successor volume.

Accordingly, the present book identifies what is so special about Hawai'i in the context of serious challenges and crises that have been confronted and resolved with the application of a very special cultural milieu. The first chapter thereby sets the tone for the rest of the volume, which covers the period up to the year 1893, when a coup topped the Kingdom of Hawai'i, and how the leaders of the coup began to reverse racial harmony from the colonization of the Islands by the United States in 1898.

After the introductory chapter, Part II identifies many serious challenges that beset the Kingdom of Hawai'i over the years, including an analysis of how they were surmounted. The early challenges were the worst, yet the responses were remarkable. Part III then describes the way in which racism entered the Islands through the intervention by outsiders – a coup in 1893.

Part IV identifies how the wisdom of the Islands could be emulated worldwide to improve race relations. Secrets of racial harmony are revealed therein.

1 The spirit of Aloha

The Archipelago of Hawai'i emerges

Volcanoes brought land to the surface of the Pacific millennia ago, producing an archipelago of some 130 islands stretching some 1,600 miles from Kure Atoll to the Island of Hawai'i (now known as the Big Island because of its size as the largest in the chain). Beginning nearly 2,000 years ago, sometime between 100–600 CE, Polynesians from the Marquesas came to Hawai'i to establish a life on the most remote archipelago on the globe. From 1000, Polynesians from Tahiti migrated to the Islands. (The term *Polynesia* comes from the Greek, meaning "many islands.")

The early peoples lived off the sea and the land, sailed far and wide, and were mostly left alone by the rest of the world, though their remarkable navigational accomplishments took them to the west coast of the North and South American continents (Buck 1953). They developed a unique culture and lived relatively harmonious and prosperous lives.

There is some evidence of Japanese explorers visiting the Islands, perhaps becoming shipwrecked, in the 1400s (Hazama and Kameji 1986). Spanish sailed into the Islands during the sixteenth century as they plied the Pacific Ocean between their colonies in North America and the Philippines. In 1527, one of three vessels in an expedition led by explorer Álvaro de Saavedra was shipwrecked; two survivors somehow made their way to Hawai'i and intermarried with the local population (Fornander 1880:ii–106). Another Spaniard, Juan Gaetano, later landed in the Islands, which in 1555 he named Las Islas de Mesa. In 1567, Álvaro Mendaña de Neira returned to map the Islands. But Japanese and Spanish kept their discovery a secret from the rest of the world. Spain wanted to establish a shipping monopoly and doubtless prevent other European powers from setting up colonies.

In 1778, however, Captain James Cook landed on one of the Islands and soon announced his finding to the world as the discovery of the "Sandwich

Islands" after his benefactor, the Earl of Sandwich. In the following century, Hawai'i offered ports of call that brought even more ships to the shores of the Islands.

The Native Hawaiians, the Kānaka Maoli, were thus exposed to peoples who followed very different norms as they docked in port. Over the years up to the present, Islanders have found that foreigners tend to have a problem in common – they do not know how to get along respectfully (cf. Boylan 1992:77).

Once upon a time, the term *Aloha Spirit* was coined to describe the very exemplary unique culture of the native peoples of Hawai'i. Although tourists and short-term visitors presume that the culture of the Islands is very simple and "laid back," they do not realize that the principles of the Aloha Spirit are very difficult to follow and can only be learned by newcomers over a period of several years of socialization, often through trial and error. There continues to be a sharp difference between the culture of the Islands and norms taken for granted in other parts of the world.

Achievements

What have the Islands accomplished that warrants such close attention? There are two types of answers. The manifest achievements do indeed deserve to be enumerated. But the underlying reasons for the successes must also be explained.

The most obvious success, of course, is the relative harmony among the various ethnic groups and races, despite challenges and tensions of various sorts over the years. Although prominent University of Hawai'i sociologist Andrew Lind (1969:97) believed that there is "no magical formula," the pages to follow reveal that magic: what is important, to be enumerated in the chapters of this book, is the normative ethos that has guided the peoples of the Islands to overcome tensions and challenges, while other parts of the world have faced the same problems as stumbling blocks to cultural, social, and political harmony. The secret of Hawai'i is *how* the people have solved those problems – both in content and in style.

One could wax eloquent about many achievements during the period since 1778. For example, the indigenous people have never initiated a "race riot" against person of other races. The Kingdom of Hawai'i was the first in the world to allow women the right to vote. The sovereign state of Hawai'i was also the first Third World country to enter the First World by no longer needing loans from elsewhere to develop a thriving economy. The palace of the monarchs was illuminated with electricity before the White House in Washington, DC. Many other "firsts" will be revealed in more detail within the chapters to follow.

Although the Kingdom of Hawaiʻi was not number one in everything, there clearly was something going on in the fabric of the society that escaped the attention of visitors hauling sandalwood from the forests, catching whales from the ocean, harvesting pineapple and sugarcane, or just sunning themselves on the beaches, while enjoying the smiling faces of those around the Islands who have every reason to be proud of the accomplishments of their land. That "something" – the spirit of Aloha – is at the core of the present volume.

The Aloha Spirit

The word *aloha* is derived from two Hawaiian words – *alo,* meaning the "front of a person," and *ha,* meaning "breath." Combined, the word describes how one person talks to another, sharing verbally and nonverbally. More eloquently, according to television personality Janet Mock, "When we are in each other's presence with the front of our bodies, we are exchanging the breath of life" (Kelleher 2015). The term *Haole*, literally "without breath," was originally used to describe a person who did not know the Hawaiian language and therefore could not communicate with the local population.

Colloquially, "aloha" manifestly means several things – hello, love, and goodbye. The latter is said with the implication that the person leaving will be missed while gone and welcomed when back. The latent content is compassion, grace, and mercy. The word is used throughout some other parts of Polynesia, such as *talofa* in Samoa, though the meaning ("What's up?") is quite different.

Yet the Aloha Spirit is not a matter of etymology, but instead a philosophy of human relations based on the culture and religion of Native Hawaiians (Handy and Pukui 1972; Kelly 1972; Howard 1974; Dudley 1990; Kameʻeleihiwa 1992; Chun 2011). Although one can describe observable cultural practices as illustrative of the Aloha Spirit, what lies behind such behavior is a monumental belief system – what cultural anthropologists and political psychologists call an "operational code" (Walker 1990). What has survived from the early Native Hawaiians was severely challenged with the introduction of capitalism and their gradual economic and political marginalization by new racial groups (Fuchs 1961:81–3; Burrows 1947; Howard 1974).

Contemporary philosophers sometimes grapple with the concept of "altruism," wishing that its practitioners would be more effective (Singer 2015). The Aloha Spirit, as more fully explicated below, is an extraordinarily effective set of culturally based norms in contrast with the rather narrow concept of altruism, which often emerges as an epiphany within individuals who have experienced mid-life crises (Brooks 2015).

The Aloha Spirit has been cited as an explanation for many practices peculiar to Hawai'i, such as the stress on community-oriented harmony, but is difficult to define and can best be understood by experience and social osmosis. A Caucasian resident of the Islands from 1823 to 1825 gives one clue of the depth of the personality of Native Hawaiians as "mild and affable in disposition, and as sprightly and active in intellect" (Stewart 1970:139–40). During those years, Caucasian missionaries from New England were having an impact on Native Hawaiians, many of whom converted to Christianity, finding Christian values compatible with the Aloha Spirit.

How can one learn how to practice the Aloha Spirit? Those born in the Islands, particularly in less populated communities, learn more easily. Newcomers to the Islands have a much more difficult time. Some can pick up the traits, but many cannot fathom that they are being judged by those who adhere to Aloha Spirit principles or how to improve their social experiences by becoming a "local" person.

Susanna Moore (2015) narrates how Lucy Thurston who viewed Hawai'i upon her arrival as a missionary in the 1820s was appalled at the "destitution, degradation, and barbarism" of what she saw. But, five decades later, she was fully accepting of and an advocate of the Aloha Spirit.

To illustrate with a contemporary example, an African American born in California recently decided to vacation in the Islands. During his trip, he flew to Moloka'i. His room in the hotel was not ready on arrival, so he sat in a chair outside, waiting patiently. Within a few minutes, a young Native Hawaiian approached him to join a volleyball game. Although the visitor said that he did not know how to play volleyball very well, his local interlocutor admitted that the players were not very good either. So he joined the game and played several rounds until his room became available. That evening he was invited to dine with the family of the players, wash dishes with others afterward, and socialize. Where else in the world would such Aloha be possible?

In contrast, another incident has been recounted by onetime Japanese legislator and Superintendent of Education Charles Toguchi. While teaching in a community in the Los Angeles area, one of his pupils was a particularly destitute African American schoolchild. He and a fellow teacher felt impelled to reach out:

Once this haole [White] teacher and I pitched in money to buy a new pair of shoes and clothes for this poor [B]lack kid who always wore old, tattered clothing to school; the next day the kid came to school with bruises on his face, dressed in his old clothes and shoes. He told us that his mother didn't believe that a [W]hite person would buy new clothes and shoes for him. So we went to the kid's home and explained everything to his mother. "Why would you do this? What do you want?" she asked. Life there was not like it was in Kahaluʻu, where people were helpful and trusted each other.

(from Cayetano 2009:300)

Because of the complexities yet the imperative of abiding by the Aloha Spirit in order to maintain a culturally rich life in the Islands, Mary Kawena Pukui (1986) decided to set down the essence in a few words:

The Aloha Spirit is the coordination of mind and heart within each person. It brings each person to the Self. Each person must think and emote good feelings to others. In the contemplation and presence of the life force, **Aloha**, the following unuhi laulā loa (free translation) may be used:

- Akahai, meaning kindness to be expressed with tenderness;
- Lōkahi, meaning unity, to be expressed with harmony;
- ʻOluʻolu, meaning agreeable, to be expressed with pleasantness;
- Haʻahaʻa, meaning humility, to be expressed with modesty;
- Ahonui, meaning patience, to be expressed with perseverance.

These are traits of character that express the charm, warmth, and sincerity of Hawaiʻi's people. It was the working philosophy of [N]ative Hawaiians and was presented as a gift to the people of Hawaiʻi.

- **Aloha** is more than a word of greeting or farewell or a salutation.
- **Aloha** means mutual regard and affection and extends warmth in caring with no obligation in return.
- **Aloha** is the essence of relationships in which each person is important to every other person for collective existence.
- **Aloha** means to hear what is not said, to see what cannot be seen and to know the unknowable.

Those who read Pukui's words may perhaps perceive that they are unattainable virtues, not suitable for the practical world of modern life, though vital in the religion of traditional Hawaiʻi. Yet over the centuries, they have served to provide a recognized standard for judging behavior, and they are still held in high esteem, though the shift in power away from Native Hawaiians diluted the influence of practitioners of the Aloha Spirit within the general population during the twentieth century. At the same time, other cultural influences merged with and reinforced the Aloha Spirit up to the present.

In 1997, Hawai'i's spiritual leader, the Reverend Abraham Akaka, died. He was the one who coined the term *the Aloha State*. Senator Daniel Akaka, his brother, eloquently summed up Native Hawaiian spirituality by quoting his father at the memorial service on September 20:

> Aloha consists of this new attitude of heart, above negativism, above legalism. It is the unconditional desire to promote the true good of other people in a friendly spirit, out of a sense of kinship. Aloha seeks to do good, with no conditions attached. We do not do good only to those who do good to us. One of the sweetest things about the love of God, about Aloha, is that it welcomes the stranger and seeks his good. A person who has the spirit of Aloha loves even when the love is not returned.
>
> (Akaka 2009:S8210–11)

Nevertheless, there is another element to the Aloha Spirit – a belief that challenges must be answered with humanistic standards of morality. The Aloha Spirit, thus, has generated practices for overcoming injustice that are of worldwide significance.

Each challenge identified in Part II was met with the Aloha Spirit. The responses were not just attitudinal, as the above formulation suggests. The Aloha Spirit is not just an idea kept inside the heads of those who adhere to the principles, but is manifest in both policy innovations and concrete actions that show sensitivity to everyone in a community.

Significance of a cultural foundation for race relations

Individuals and nations make choices based on their fundamental cultural belief systems in responding to daily or extraordinary situations. While some academic social scientists have long focused on the centrality of culture as an underlying explanation for patterns of national behavior (Schneider and Bonjean 1973; cf. Schafer and Walker 2006), others leave out cultural elements as a sort of "black box." Invoking culture to explain the basis for individual and societal choices nevertheless reveals intervening elements that are otherwise impossible to explain:

Challenges → Culture → Responses

In many respects, the cultural norms found in Hawai'i are quite distinct from that of the rest of the world. Indeed, many in the Islands today reject crass elements of what is sometimes called "American culture." Norms govern behavior, though culture is shaped by experience, by trial and error, in adapting to circumstances.

To understand how the Aloha Spirit originated, survived in the face of adversity, and was maintained in the increasingly multiethnic Island environment of the nineteenth century, a review of challenges and responses is therefore necessary. That is the aim of Part II, where situations that led to disaster in other parts of the world, including the clash between competing cultures that now strains Iraq and many parts of the world, are identified as resulting in progress in Hawai'i.

Part II

Historic challenges to the Kingdom of Hawai'i

Hawai'i was isolated from most of the world until 1778, when Captain James Cook decided to broadcast the existence of the Islands to the world. Thereafter, a deluge of problems arose. The following challenged the political and social order:

- civil wars
- arrival of diseases from abroad, decimating the indigenous population
- efforts to conquer and colonize the islands by foreign powers
- religious conflicts
- environmental despoliation
- transformation from feudalism to capitalism
- overexploitation of workers
- foreigners overwhelm natives
- discrimination by foreigners based on race and sex
- civil riots and attempted coups

What country in the world could have faced any of these problems without imploding? The next chapters describe challenges up to the coup of 1893, which brought down the curtain on the remarkable advances achieved by the Kingdom of Hawai'i that must not be forgotten.

2   Civil wars

From disunity to unity

When Captain James Cook docked at a port on the Island of Kauaʻi in 1778, a civil war was already in progress (Daws 1968:ch2). Civil conflicts involving the chiefs of the four major islands – Kauaʻi, Oʻahu, Maui and Hawaiʻi – had been going on for some time. During wartime in the Islands, there was a custom to stop battles in a manner similar to the Truce of God established by Catholic Europe in the year 1027: armed combat was disallowed during Island holidays, and one side could signal to the other to quit for a day in order to attend to the wounded.

Many wars over the years developed a warrior class (Fornander 1880). Each time a military leader died on one island, property was redistributed by his successors, resulting in considerable economic and political instability within each island (Hitch 1992:ch1).

Efforts to bring unity also occurred. In the fourteenth century, for example, there is a record of an invasion of Oʻahu by forces from Maui. In 1738, the chief of the island of Hawaiʻi had an alliance with his brother, who controlled the island of Maui. Together they subdued the smaller island of Molokaʻi as a stepping stone toward subjugation of the island of Oʻahu. When the ruler of Oʻahu readied his troops for a bloody battle, they reconsidered their design to unify the islands. In the Treaty of Naonealaʻa that year, the three rulers agreed to a peace in which any future bilateral war could be vetoed by the third ruler. They had in effect established a security council.

But new rulers came to the fore by 1759, when Maui and Hawaiʻi fought each other. Soon, forces from Hawaiʻi controlled eastern Maui. Kahekili of Maui retaliated against Hawaiʻi and also sought to annex Oʻahu. Fighting continued until 1782, when Kahekili subdued Oʻahu and took up residence in Honolulu. But that left a power vacuum on Maui.

Although the Big Island had been unified in the early eighteenth century, civil war broke out in 1782, when the successor to the chief fell ill and died.

His brother sought to redistribute land contrary to the interest of the chiefs of the Kohala and Kona sides of the island. Kamehameha, nephew of the former chief, then mobilized troops and launched a civil war.

The principal reason for Kamehameha's eventual victory was not only that he had a certain amount of charisma and energy. He owed much to the British. Captain Cook, who landed on Maui later in 1778, met Kahekili, and proceeded in early 1779 to the island of Hawai'i not far from Kona. Although Cook was primarily an explorer, he armed his ship's crew with firearms in case of pirates. Cook at first befriended Kalani'ōpu'u but later decided to take him as a hostage in order to retrieve small boats stolen by some of the natives. As a result, a scuffle ensued in which Cook died, though by stabbing, not bullets.

When the chiefs saw the power of Cook's firearms, particularly cannons, they sought to acquire them as more ships landed to obtain such supplies as food and water to continue their journeys in the Pacific. In early 1790, a ship sailed into Kamehameha's domain and was captured, providing him with a storehouse of weapons. That gave him the edge in the civil war with his uncle, as well as with Kahekili. Soon, he conquered Maui, Moloka'i, and the smaller Island of Lana'i, and then solidified control over the Big Island.

Kamehameha instituted the Māmalahoe Kānāwai, the Law of the Splintered Paddle: "Let every elderly person, woman, and child lie by the roadside in safety." Without knowledge of the Synod of Charroux in 989, he was replicating the Pax Dei (the Peace of God). The impetus was that during 1782, while his foot was caught in a rock, he had been hit with a paddle, which broke into pieces. Kamehameha was then left unconscious as if dead. In 1794, when the two perpetrators were brought before him, he proclaimed the law in determining their fate: King Kamehameha instead blamed himself for attacking innocent people in the past, gave the two men gifts of land, and set them free.

From 1780 to 1800, Hawai'i was a frequent stopover location in the otter and seal fur trade between North America and China. For the route from Canada to Australia, Hawai'i was in a strategic location. George Vancouver, who sailed to Hawai'i on several occasions in the late eighteenth century, was astonished when one of the chiefs, named Kamehameha, sought an alliance with Britain so as to prevail in the civil war with rival chiefs on the various islands. Kamehameha even offered to cede the island of Hawai'i to Britain. Although the Union Jack went up in 1794, London was more concerned with European matters, and the flag soon came down (Kuykendall 1938:41).

Kamehameha next set his sights on O'ahu. Fighting continued until 1795, when his army achieved victory by pushing Kahekili's forces to the precipice of Pali in the Battle of Nu'uanu. Kamehameha then controlled all islands but Kaua'i and Ni'ihau, which were under the control of Kaumauli'i. Kamehameha's navy twice tried to conquer Kaua'i, but they were turned back by stormy seas, so he decided to consolidate rule over the rest of the islands rather than achieving immediate full unification. He then established a monarchical form of government.

In 1796, a group of Russians established a trading post on Kaua'i with Kaumauli'i's encouragement. Also in 1796, Nāmākēhā revolted on the Island of Hawai'i, seeking to take control of the island in Kamehameha's absence. The king then postponed a second conquest of Kaua'i to return home in order to put down the insurrection.

Kamehameha then remained on his home island for the rest of the century to consolidate his rule. Kailua-Kona on that island, known colloquially as the Big Island because its size dwarfs the other islands, thus became the first capital of all the islands. Kamehameha then appointed governors for all the islands but Kaua'i and Ni'ihau. Kamehameha maintained unified rule, thereby ending land redistribution formerly at the whim of military leaders.

Kamehameha the Great, as he is now known, shifted the capital several times. In 1804, he moved the royal family from Kailua-Kona to Waikīkī, and then to Honolulu during 1809, in preparation to wrest control of Kaua'i and Ni'ihau from Kaumauli'i.

But in 1810, Kaumauli'i decided to voluntarily surrender. Kamehameha then appointed him governor of both Kaua'i and Ni'ihau. With imperial powers snapping up island territories in the Pacific, Kamehameha provided a sense of security through unity. In 1812, he went back to Kailua-Kona, the home ground of the royal family.

There were no visible hard feelings over his conquest, though in 1815 Kaumauli'i secretly asked a German commercial representative from a Russian company for assistance in taking control over the Islands (Daws 1968:51–2). But the proposal was later disavowed by a Russian government representative. In 1816, Kamehameha commissioned the country's flag, a combination of American stripes with the Union Jack of Britain in place of the stars.

When the Russians withdrew from their trading posts on Kaua'i during 1818, Kamehameha was in full control. He reigned through a Council of Chiefs and appointed his queen, Ka'ahumanu as kuhina-nui, a position similar to premier. He was emulating the British form of monarchical government, which has never had a constitutional document.

Outcome of the civil wars

Conditions from the arrival of Captain Cook were comparatively benign. The civil war was relatively restrained. Kamehameha's victory was accepted without bitterness as he established a monarchical form of government, unifying the laws of the Islands while granting power to governors in each island grouping. Thus, the agreeableness of the Aloha Spirit so moderated civil wars that there was little lust for revenge in Hawaiʻi. Although civil wars have torn apart many countries over the centuries, such as Korea, the outcome in Hawaiʻi was harmonious acceptance of the unification of the Islands.

Kamehameha's first-born son, crowned Kamehameha II when his father died in 1819, shifted the capital to Lahainā on Maui in 1820, an important port when trade boomed in sandalwood and whaling. But in 1845, trade became more lucrative in Honolulu, where Kamehameha III moved the royal family to establish the new seat of government. In the next decades, the government was increasingly influenced by Caucasian interests that benefited from the trade.

Thus, Hawaiʻi survived a challenge that has rarely been overcome elsewhere around the world. Even in Southern states of the United States, a sense of divisiveness lingers, as evidenced by hate groups that carry on the animus of the Civil War (Widmer 2015). Discussion about removing the flag of the Confederate states from the state capitols in the South did not go onto the public agenda until 2015 after a White supremacist gunned down parishioners engaging in Bible study at a famous Black church in Charleston, South Carolina, whereupon other parishioners publicly forgave the culprit – showing altruism akin to the Aloha Spirit.

Today, chagrin over the fall of the monarchy in 1893 remains, but that is an amazing story told later in this volume. Native Hawaiians may have surrendered politically, but they will never relinquish their amiable nature.

3   Epidemics

Early diseases

Before Western contact, the Native Hawaiian population was extraordinarily robust (Snow 1974), but something intervened to reduce resistance: diseases came from trading ships, which brought infected persons to the Islands.

When European ships began to dock after 1778, some on board carried diseases. Germs quickly spread to those who greeted them on the islands of Kaua'i and Ni'ihau. In late 1778, Cook spotted venereal disease among the native peoples on Maui, and the same observation occurred when he docked on the island of Hawai'i in early 1779 (Daws 1968:6, 9, 32). The disease had presumably spread from Kaua'i or perhaps was a legacy of the stopovers of Spanish ships from the sixteenth century. But Cook had medicines to treat their sores. In any case, venereal disease is spread through intimate, not casual contact, so no epidemic was created from what some around the world have unflatteringly called the "English disease." More serious diseases, previously unknown in the Islands, were spread as more visitors arrived in the Islands during the nineteenth century.

Serious diseases

Traders sought cash crops – at first sandalwood from the upland forests and later whales from the adjacent ocean. Both brought an economic boom to the Islands. Accustomed to farming in the moderate oceanfront climate, commoners were soon conscripted by chiefs to go to the cool mountains to cut down trees, first for sandalwood and later to collect firewood for the whalers. As a result, they became exhausted from the work and the exposure to the elements (Kuykendall 1938:89; Hitch 1992:42). The whaling trade brought visitors for months at a time, as there was an interval between the season for hunting in the south and the north (Hitch 1992:41).

Cholera was the source of the first epidemic, taking a toll of 175,000 lives during 1803–1804 (PCA 1864). Between 1832 and 1834, some 10,000 lost their lives in an epidemic of unknown origin, possibly malaria (PCA 1864; Daws 1968:87). Measles, whooping-cough, and influenza claimed another 10,000 from 1848 to 1849 (The Friend 1849). Another 5,000 perished from smallpox in 1853 (PCA 1864). Leprosy struck in 1865. Bubonic plague emerged in 1899, but was limited to Chinatowns in Honolulu and Kahalui, Maui. In 1903, dengue fever cases arose, and yellow fever broke out in 1911 (Hope and Hope 2003).

Coping with diseases

During the fourteenth century, the Black Plague of Europe gave rise to anti-Semitism due to accusations that the epidemic was brought to Europe by Jews, who in turn were massacred in many towns and villages (Bennett and Hollister 2006:329–30). No such hysteria afflicted Hawai'i, although Caucasians disembarking in the ports of the Islands were the source of the diseases.

Traditionally, Hawai'i used the method of the quarantine (the kapu) to isolate those who fell sick. Native Hawaiians used the method with the expectation that victims would persevere until cured. Islanders relied on kahuna priests to handle illnesses, but they were unable to cope with the new situation. They believed that certain new foods were responsible, but that was not the answer. For many diseases, including leprosy, there was no alternative but isolation from the population. Thus, ships were held up in the port of Honolulu during 1836 to ensure that they would not spread smallpox. Hawai'i's quarantine law passed in 1839, nearly fifty years before a similar law in the United States.

The judgment has often been made that Native Hawaiians lacked the antibodies to cope with the diseases, whereas Europeans had developed a certain amount of immunity, built up over centuries, to survive various illnesses (Schmitt and Nordyke 2001:3). Another explanation is that modern public health institutions did not initially exist to mitigate the outbreaks.

When presented with up-to-date medical procedures, the native population showed Aloha toward new methods of disease control, notably vaccines. New arrivals from New England brought vaccines, but their supply was insufficient, and often the vaccines were too crudely made (Schmitt and Nordyke 2001:140). In 1822, the first water filtration plant was established (Hope and Hope 2003), and a medical school was set up on an emergency basis in 1828.

In 1851, Hawai'i's government became the first country in the world to establish a Board of Health; elsewhere, institutions of public health came later. In addition, Queen's Hospital (now Medical Center) was established in 1859 for the care of Native Hawaiians who were falling victim to the various epidemic diseases; the facility continues operation in the present.

In 1866, those with leprosy were removed to Kalawao, an extremely inaccessible part of Moloka'i Island. A Sanitary Commission was set up in 1862. A Food Commission was launched in 1899, and sewer construction began in 1899.

Impact of epidemics

Depopulation of indigenous peoples by plagues introduced by Europeans was widespread in the Americas, Southern Africa, Australasia, and the Pacific Islands (McNeill 1976; Diamond 1997; Francis 2005). The situation in Hawai'i was no different. In 1778, there were about 300,000 Native Hawaiians or possibly 800,000, but there were only 38,000 by 1900 (Nordyke 1989:178–9, 183; Stannard 1989:30; Hitch 1992:19; Kane 1997:68).

Depopulation resulting from the epidemics was not the only problem for Native Hawaiians. Panic over the deaths disrupted community tranquility (Schmitt and Nordyke 2001:140–1). For example, as his chiefs and soldiers died, Kamehameha canceled voyages intended to subdue resistance to his rule on Kaua'i (Schmitt and Nordyke 2001:43). Lacking stable communities, many ecosystems were left unattended (Wilcox and Maly 2010). Accordingly, the monarchs encouraged interracial marriage, as the loss of life through epidemics caused them to fear that the Native Hawaiian race was otherwise doomed to extinction (Geschwender 1982:208–9). Nevertheless, only about 10 percent of the population of the Islands was racially mixed by the end of the century (Schmitt 1965).

By 1890, the indigenous population was a minority in its own land (Nordyke 1989). Meanwhile, the Caucasian community, which constituted less than 100 in 1820, numbered 29,000 by 1900 (Nordyke 1989), while thousands of Chinese and Japanese sugarcane workers were cultivating fields once farmed by the native population.

In short, the response to the diseases was to invoke the long-practiced technique of the quarantine, accept medical assistance from outside, and establish new government institutions to regularize control of diseases – showing kindness rather than zerosum thinking. Advice from the Islands might have served to mitigate the severity of the Black Plague in fourteenth-century Europe, when an innovation by Venice – the quarantine, a word coined by Italians – was to force ships to stay in port for a period of forty days before disembarking.

Yet the resulting depopulation increased the threat of a colonial takeover. The kingdom, nevertheless, was able to establish itself as a fully sovereign state by applying the Aloha Spirit to foreign relations, as indicated next.

4 The threat of colonization

Colonialism in the Pacific

Imperial land grabs and subsequent drawing of artificial boundaries have scarred much of contemporary Africa, where civil wars have been endemic. After the era of exploration from Columbus to Cook, however, European colonial powers were not particularly eager to annex territories in the Pacific, which had few lucrative assets and were reasonably receptive to trade. Various countries send ships to the Pacific during the nineteenth century. After the British did so, Kamehameha I and II believed that the kingdom had an alliance with Britain (Hitch 1992:32–3).

Russian ships first visited Kaua'i in 1796, during the last year of the reign of Catherine the Great. Small Russia trading posts were soon established on Kaua'i, but the venture was abandoned by 1818. In 1816, after docking in port from 1809, Russians began to construct a fort near Honolulu harbor. When Kamehameha learned of the development, he dispatched members of his army to confront workers at the site, whereupon the Russians stopped construction, although they continued to trade until 1826 (Barrett 1988).

An American warship in docked in 1814, and in 1826 the king signed his first treaty – with the United States. The agreement granted most-favored-nation access to trade with the Islands and also arranged for the government to pay debts owed to American merchants (Kuykendall 1938:435; Stauffer 1983). In 1836, the government signed an agreement with Britain, promising never to prosecute British citizens, and France secured a similar arrangement in 1839.

Sometime in the 1840s, Kamehameha III adopted the Code of Etiquette of the Congress of Vienna to conduct international diplomacy in order to handle local business conflicts before they led to an international incident.

Foreigners seeking to get rich in the Islands wanted the monarchy to grant them special favors or at least to enforce contracts that were not being followed. If their demands were not met, they sometimes contacted their consular officials in town, who in turn would go to court. In 1842, nevertheless, the British consul left Honolulu for London to present grievances: rent for a land that he had presumably leased was not being paid by the tenants, and he was told that the lease was invalid. His deputy then plotted to obtain British colonization of Hawai'i. In 1843, Kamehameha III discussed the possibility of joint annexation by France and the United States with representatives from the two countries but instead decided to sign an agreement with Lord George Paulet, commander of a newly arrived British warship, to cede sovereignty to Britain with the stipulation that the Kingdom of Hawai'i would later get back its independence. Paulet even imposed taxes, relaxed liquor laws, repealed the law against fornication, and otherwise pretended to be the new governor general. But when London got word of the agreement, interest in colonizing the Islands was disavowed. Paulet sailed away six months later. Britain and France instead signed a noncolonization agreement in 1843, recognizing the Kingdom of Hawai'i as a sovereign state (ibid.:206–21).

Next, two envoys from the king went to Washington to make the agreement trilateral. One suggested that otherwise the king might cede sovereignty to Britain. In response, President John Tyler agreed in 1843 to join the two European powers, implicitly extending the Monroe Doctrine to Hawai'i (Stevens 1945:18–20; Daws 1968:118; Geschwender 1982:195). The entente of 1843 between Britain, France, and the United States was premised in part on the view that diplomacy was the preferred method for conflict resolution on matters of disputes in local and international trade.

The main reason for lack of interest in colonization by the major powers was that the kingdom had progressively adopted capitalism and was eager to trade. Except for Japan and Thailand, which also quickly embraced capitalism in the ports of Bangkok and Tokyo, imperial takeovers were thought necessary elsewhere throughout Asia and the Pacific in order to overcome active resistance to capitalism.

France's first colony in the Pacific came during 1843 – a protectorate in the Society Islands, with a capital in Tahiti. After the Tahitians declared independence, France mobilized forces and prevailed in a war from 1844 to 1847.

Persecution of Catholics by Protestant missionaries in Hawai'i, as described in the following chapter, was a pretext for colonization in 1849, when French Admiral Louis Tromelin presented ten demands to the king. Three days later, the demands were not met, so he ordered the landing of 140 French marines. They then captured Honolulu Fort, raided government and private buildings, and seized the king's personal yacht. Although the French government later disavowed the action, they never compensated the kingdom for the damages (Charlot 1970). Two weeks later, having met no armed resistance, Tromelin sailed away. The yacht went to Tahiti and was never returned.

In 1851, when relations with Paris remained tense, Kamehameha III was authorized by his legislature to become a protectorate of the United States and even raise the American flag in the event of future hostilities with France (Kuykendall 1938:392–5). Most advisers to the king were Americans, and most trade was exchanged with the United States. But the protectorate was never implemented. In 1853, a treaty of annexation that would make Hawai'i a state was drawn up by American residents, but Washington would not agree (Kuykendall 1938:423). Kamehameha IV, who acceded to the throne in 1854, then opposed annexation, preferring a trade treaty with the United States. In 1867, an annexation treaty was under discussion again, but Congress was still not interested.

Meanwhile, France established a colony in tin-rich New Caledonia in 1853; Hawai'i had no equivalent resource to mine. The United States offered to buy Midway from Hawai'i, but when the king declined, the atoll was seized anyway during 1867. Fiji and the Tokelau Islands became Britain's first colonies in the South Pacific during 1877. In the 1880s, Germany began looking for colonies, and snapped up New Guinea in 1884. But the European imperialists left Hawai'i out of the land grab, preferring to establish formal diplomatic relations instead.

Colonial threats subside

Native Hawaiians realized that they could now develop pride in a national identity that would differ from that of Britain, France, the United States, and other countries. King Kalākaua, who ruled from 1874 to 1891, brought back the hula and traditional chants that earlier had been frowned upon by the missionaries. In 1876, he replaced a national anthem with Christian overtones to the current refrain, *Hawai'i Ponō'i*.

During a visit to sixteen countries around the world that began in 1880, Kalākaua sought an alliance with Japan by offering the hand of his daughter Princess Ka'iulani to Prince Komatsu. However, the emperor declined. He was the first reigning monarchy to circumnavigate the globe and the first foreign head of state to speak before a joint session of Congress (hawaiilife. com). In 1883, he sent a proclamation to twenty-six governments, asking them to stop colonizing in the Pacific, and in 1886, he even asked Washington to cede Midway back as an integral part of the Hawaiian archipelago (Daws 1968:235–6). In 1887, he negotiated a treaty of confederation with one of the rival factions in Samoa, but the other faction made a deal with Germany and became a colony ruled from Berlin. Little did he know that he would be confronted by a major coup in 1887 that would set the stage for an eventual transformation of the independent country into a colony of the United States. That story is told in Part III of the present volume.

In short, for nearly fifty years after the confrontation with the French, no foreign power sought to make the Islands into a colony, while imperial powers gobbled up the rest of the Pacific. Hawai'i was an accepted independent state within the international system, exchanging ambassadors, conducting foreign relations, and adopting treaties. Aloha displayed for the early visitors and their religious beliefs was extended to the countries of the world.

5 Religious conflicts

The traditional Hawaiian religion

For centuries, Native Hawaiians developed a religion that honored nature. Principles of the Aloha Spirit were derived from their religion. They particularly honored Pelehonuamea, the goddess of the volcano – known as Pele for short. When Captain Cook and personnel aboard trading ships arrived, they undertook no effort to destroy their religion or to impose another.

But foreigners brought all sorts of debauchery and misconduct to the Islands, violating various prohibitions in the native religion. The kahunas were proved wrong in predicting that the gods would retaliate against miscreants for scandalous behavior, such as violence following the overconsumption of alcohol. The Hawaiian gods did not wreak vengeance as expected.

In 1819, Kamehameha I's favorite queen, Kaʻahumanu, persuaded Kamehameha II to decree an end of the kapu (taboo) system – that is, the practice of declaring various locations or practices off limits. For example, there was a kapu on women eating with men. She thereby undermined those who wanted to use their religious positions in order to buttress their claims to the throne (McGregor and Aluli 2014:n1).

Thus, the nineteenth century began with a spirit of liberation – including women's liberation – from past injustice based on religion. There was a new sense of unity between the sexes. She thereby paved the way for the arrival of a new faith.

Christianity arrives in two forms

In 1809, while civil war was ongoing, a Native Hawaiian named Opukahaʻia and his friend Hopu hopped onto an American ship to avoid being captured in a battle. The ship took them to Connecticut, where Opukahaʻia learned English, started developing a Romanized version of the Hawaiian language, and converted to Christianity. He entreated the American Board of Commissioners for Foreign Missions to go to Hawai'i, but alas, he died before they got organized. In 1820, the first group of about a dozen Protestant Congregational missionaries and their families arrived, mostly from New England (Daws 1968:62). The entourage included four Native Hawaiians, including Hopu, who had also been educated at the Foreign Mission School (Daws 1968:63; U.S. Departments of Interior and Justice 2000:22). Their goal, to convert the indigenous population to their faith, introduced the first religious challenge.

The missionaries not only preached the Gospel, but also criticized traditional cultural practices that they deemed offensive, such as public nudity (even while surfing), polygamy, royal incest, and even the hula, which they considered too sensual. Nevertheless, they had to approach the rulers of each island to gain acceptance in order to build mission houses and schools, while seeking to attract commoners. The nobility and monarchy accepted the new faith in part as an opportunity reassert norms of moderation from the Hawaiian religion. Drunken brawls had shocked the people, and the early Protestants branded all such drinking as immoral. Ka'ahumanu accepted Protestantism, and many Native Hawaiians followed her example.

Although the "moral wars" (Daws 1968:87–91) conducted by the missionaries included an effort to ban alcohol and drunkenness, Native Hawaiians enjoyed both Christianity and alcohol and tried their best to avoid drunkenness because of a traditional belief that all behavior should be moderate, one of the components of the Aloha Spirit.

The cholera epidemic of 1803–1804 had so disrupted life in the Islands that the missionaries were able to exploit the turmoil by preaching new meaning to life. In 1824, a missionary leader insisted that everyone observe the Sabbath by refraining from lighting fires, traveling, or working (ibid.:72). Ka'ahumanu, who agreed with the Protestant's objections to adultery, fornication, intemperance, and other misconduct, tried to impose fines for such misconduct (ibid.:83). The missionaries believed that Christian teaching insisted that good people wear considerable clothing to protect the modesty of their bodies, and they undertook to dismantle the Hawaiian polytheistic religion as idolatrous.

Then in 1827, a small number of French Catholic missionaries also appeared. The second religious challenge emerged because the Congregationalist missionaries objected to Catholicism, which used wine in the communion ceremony. Although the Protestants tried to dissuade the native population from accepting a different form of Christianity, O'ahu Governor Boki attended Catholic mass that year. After Boki died in 1830, Protestant chiefs sought to ban Catholicism. In 1831, those who attended mass were jailed or sentenced to hard labor; priests were also seized and ordered to depart. While mass Protestant baptisms occurred during the 1830s (Meller 1958:798), the practice of Catholicism went underground.

Anti-Catholic measures provoked a strong reaction: in 1839, the captain of a French ship, Cyrille Laplace, sailed to Hawai'i, threatening to make war over the discrimination against Catholics. He also demanded abolition of the tariff on French cognac and wine.

Religious toleration

Kamehameha III thereupon agreed to stop anti-Catholic persecution, never to prosecute French citizens, and to allow Catholic churches to operate. In 1839, he chose religious toleration as the Hawaiian way to resolve the conflict by issuing the Edict of Toleration, which was incorporated into the constitution adopted in 1840.

Once both Catholics and Protestants were accepted, the door was open for other religions to arrive in the Islands and enjoy peaceful acceptance, though after 1854 none were allowed to operate sectarian schools with more than twenty-five pupils. Chinese, recruited to work on the sugarcane plantations in the 1850s, brought Buddhist, Confucian, and Taoist practices. Mormon missionaries and Jews began to enter in the 1850s. Japanese laborers brought various sects of Buddhism and Shintoism in the 1880s, eventually erecting more than 100 shrines and temples. Islam did not make its way to the Islands until after statehood. Religious tolerance was based on the desire to promote harmony.

Yet Protestant missionaries would often preach one message on Sundays and engage in discriminatory practices during the rest of the week. One such person, the Reverend Charles Hyde, was the subject of a novella by onetime Honolulu visitor Robert Louis Stevenson – *The Strange Case of Dr. Jekyll and Mr. Hyde* (1886). Stevenson was shocked that Hyde denigrated the saintly efforts of Father Damien (born Jozef De Veuster in Belgium) to come to the aid of those with Hansen's Disease (leprosy) by living with them, thereby exposing himself to the disease. Hyde and other missionaries also opposed interracial marriage (Porteus 1962:161, 324; Daws 1968:114). Christianity, nevertheless, flourished in the Islands.

Unfortunately, a similar spirit of Aloha toward competing religions has not motivated those in the contemporary Middle East. In contrast with the concept of Aloha toward diverse religions, wars based on religion are tearing apart the Middle East in the present day.

6   Environmental despoliation

Damage to the environment was inevitable as the economy changed from self-sufficient food gathering to plantation agriculture. Native Hawaiians managed their environment in exemplary ways, but foreign capitalists were less interested in preserving delicate ecosystems.

Early environmental changes

According to a proverb held fast by Native Hawaiians, "The land is the chief; man is the servant." Native Hawaiians brought various species to the Islands when they arrived in prehistoric times. Forests and brush were often burned to clear the land for agriculture (Culleney 2006). Chicken and pigs were integrated into the ecosystems. Later, sweet potatoes were imported from the Americas. The environment then began to show limits (Cabin 2013:xxiv–xxvi). Species brought in the seventh century killed species that previously had no predators (Moore 2015). The world's largest adz quarry, consisting of stones fashioned into cutting tools, operated in 1100 but was later discontinued (and then rediscovered in 1975).

An effective method of conservation was the kapu applied to the environment. Native Hawaiians recognized that limits on animal slaughter, fish catches, and vegetable harvests were needed to allow replenishment.

In about 1100–1200, possibly associated with second wave of Polynesian migration, a new environmental concept of conservation arose with particular attention to maintaining the flow of water from the mountains to the sea through irrigation ditches so that taro would be irrigated and fishponds could thrive (Connelly 2014:91). Land was held in common by rulers on each island, who delegated maintenance to the chiefs. Farmers were allowed to live in slivers of land, known as ahupuaʻa, around streams running from the mountains toward the sea so long as they were productive in the opinion of the chiefs on each island.

After 1200, travel back and forth across Polynesia stopped. Two possible reasons are that forests for making sailing vessels had been exhausted or that large birds aiding navigation had been eaten to virtual extinction (Cabin 2013:xxiii–xiv). To provide green, red, and yellow capes for the nobility, thousands of birds had been killed (Moore 2015).

The diligence of the agricultural workers impressed the first foreigners. In contrast, Native Hawaiians viewed the early Caucasian visitors as lazy (Daws 1968:49). According to some observers, the ecosystem in 1778 was one of the most efficient, self-contained agricultural production systems in the world because of the high-yielding taro ponds, dry land agricultural systems, fishponds, and water catchment systems (Handy 1965; Handy and Pukui 1972; Diamond 1997). When Captain Cook arrived, he sought and obtained plentiful food and water.

New species after Captain Cook

Although the pristine ecosystem was challenged by new species brought by the first settlers, the Polynesian travelers learned how to introduce new species without ecological disaster. Accordingly, there was little resistance to the entry of new animals and plants from the Western world during the nineteenth century.

The port of Honolulu became a convenient place for trading ships to stop, gain some rest from transoceanic travel, and obtain supplies. In 1793, British explorer George Vancouver brought cattle to the Islands to satisfy the taste of his crews. Despite the building of fences and walls around the new livestock, ecosystem damage occurred due to overgrazing and trampling (Wilcox and Maly 2010). The introduction of cattle, deer, goats, horses, pigs, and sheep damaged ferns, grasses, trees, and vines that had blessed Islanders for centuries (Moore 2015). Many hillsides became barren (Tummons 2010:164).

Thousands of animal and plant species in Hawai'i are found nowhere else. The arrival of outsiders jeopardized the delicate ecological balance. One-third of the bird species disappeared from 1778 to the present; animal and plant extinctions exceed all other states in the United States (Tobin and Higuchi 1992:124).

While foreigners prospected for cash crops, one initially turned up to have a prized commercial value – sandalwood. Chinese were keenly interested, and in 1810 Kamehameha allowed three American traders to conscript Native Hawaiians to harvest logs from the sandalwood forest. The first shipment to Canton was in 1812, but within eighteen years, the forest was depleted. As a result, a law was passed in 1839 to restrict cutting of the resource. When that failed to stop the practice, Kamehameha III in 1846 nationalized all forests – that is, they became government property. But that was too late to save sandalwood, which grows no more in Hawai'i. In the frenzy to cut sandalwood, traditional agriculture was neglected, and the price of food soared (Hitch 1992:39).

In 1821, whaling grounds were discovered in the North Pacific, so ships began to dock in the port of Honolulu. Five years later, a whaler on Maui dumped a barrel of water containing mosquitoes. Although humans got used to coping with the pests, birds did not, so they moved to higher elevations (Tummons 2010:164).

From the 1830s, the Island economy was dominated by commercial whale hunting to obtain oil from blubber for lighting the lamps of the world. Whales seasonally accustomed to being sheltered in the Islands were then indiscriminately slaughtered (Lebo 2010; cf. Morehead 1966). The whalers also sought firewood, which further depleted the forests and left agriculture unattended (Hitch 1992:41–2). The whalers were accustomed to white potatoes, which were then introduced as a mini-cash crop.

In 1859, the discovery of petroleum at Titusville, Pennsylvania, doomed the whaling industry: by 1871, kerosene was an inexpensive substitute for whale oil, and later gasoline powered motorcars. But during the era of the kingdom, the energy of the Islands was self-sufficiently derived from biomass, bagasse (sugarcane waste), and hydropower (Curtis 2010:179).

The most important natural resource of the Islands has been the amazingly fertile land. Sugarcane, grown and chewed by the early Polynesians, was first milled in 1802 by a Chinese merchant (Deerr 1949). The first major sugar plantation began operation in 1835. By the 1870s, sugarcane rose to become the number one cash crop in the Islands. Pineapple, first introduced in 1813 by Kamehameha's Spanish advisor Don Francisco de Paula y Marín, was abundant by the 1890s. To make way for the new crops, land was cleared, interrupting traditional plots – that is, the ahupua'a that stretched from upslope forests to the sea alongside streams. Damage to the ecosystems by new agricultural crops and disturbances in the fish supplies were noticeably taking their toll by the 1860s.

Water crisis and solution

During the 1860s, elaborate irrigation systems for sugarcane cultivation, requiring two tons of water for each pound of sugar (HSPA 1926:48), also interfered with the flow of streams for those who grew other agricultural crops, driving local farmers out of business (Blaisdell, Minton, and Hasager 2014:298). The result was a water shortage crisis in the 1870s. Sugarcane producers then took the lead in demanding action from the monarchy (Cabin 2013:24–5).

In response to the water problem, which confronted both native farmers and sugarcane producers, the government established a Commission of Private Ways and Water Rights in 1860. With two Native Hawaiians on the three-member board, conflicts were resolved in favor of the indigenous people (Sproat 2010:190). Thus, measures by Native Hawaiians averted disaster.

Eradication methods

Problems arose when rats jumped from merchant ships into the Island environment. British scientist W. B. Espeut brought the mongoose from Jamaica in 1883 to deal with rats, but the new predatory animal became an even more serious pest – especially after the discovery that mongooses are diurnal, eating only a few rats during the day, whereas rats are largely nocturnal.

More successful was the later import of insects that checked the borer and the leaf hopper, which raised havoc in sugarcane fields (Hitch 1992:77). The Kingdom of Hawai'i, in other words, made advances in what was later called the field of tropical agriculture.

Conclusion

Elsewhere around the world, ecological despoliation has had more calamitous consequences. The most famous case is the fate of the Easter Islanders. Scholars have attributed soil erosion leading to drought as the reason for the decline of the Mayas in the tenth century (Dunning and Beach 1994). Excessive deforestation evidently doomed the Minoan civilization on Crete during the fifteenth century (Perlin 2005). In contrast, sensible measures by Native Hawaiians averted disaster.

7 Transformation from feudalism to capitalism

"Primitive communism"

Self-sufficient agriculture prevailed when the first Polynesians reached Hawai'i. Karl Marx's model of "primitive communism" was based on early anthropological accounts from the Islands (Morgan 1870; Engels 1884; Harris 1968), though there is evidence is that some parts of the Islands were more individualistic (Handy and Handy 1972). Prosperity reined almost everywhere, thanks to amazingly productive land for agriculture and an ocean with bountiful fish supplies.

Feudalism declines

When Captain Cook arrived, the economic arrangement in force was feudalism. The land was organized into watershed districts, known as ahupua'a. Polynesians arriving in the eleventh century had imposed semi-despotic control in which a nobility (ali'i) from Tahiti assigned commoners (maka'āinana), descendants of the original Marquesans, to the food-gathering tasks of agriculture and fishing (Kamakau 1964:3; Finney 1973:13–14; Lindo and Mower 1980:21; Blaisdell, Minton, and Hasager 2014:291). However, recurrent civil war made the arrangement somewhat unstable.

Cook brought barter capitalism to the Islands, as his men traded with the commoners for food and water in exchange for modern technological products, including weapons (Kamakau 1976:34; Beechert 1985:10–11). The enthusiasm with which Native Hawaiians sought to engage in barter trade is well recorded in the accounts of Captain Cook's voyages. Islanders demonstrated entrepreneurial talent by acquiring iron and other commodities carried aboard ships.

Contact with the artifacts of Western civilization soon whetted the appetite of Kamehameha and the ali'i to purchase fine clothing and instruments of modern technology (Sahlins 1958:1, 412). To obtain Western commodities, the ali'i quickly established a monopoly on foreign trade in sandalwood to enrich their coffers (Wilkes 1845:iv, 218; Ralston 1978:128–9). Kamehameha I then nationalized all foreign trade, and foreign traders offered $200,000 credit to the monarchy as an advance on the purchase of sandalwood logs. But when the supply was exhausted, the creditors called in their loans, leaving no alternative for the government but to impose onerous taxes on the people (Kuykendall 1938:91–2). The debt was not settled until 1843, thanks to the first treaty with the United States: the monarchy arranged for trade concessions with the United States in exchange for having Washington cancel the amount due (Kuykendall 1938:435; Stauffer 1983).

The commerce-minded foreigners (Haoles, a term now applied to Caucasians or Whites) lusted to control the economy of the archipelago. After sandalwood, the principal industry was to service whaling ships and their crews, who docked in port from the 1820s.

The kings held all land in common, parceling land out to the ali'i, and commoners were allowed to live on land that they used productively. Yet there was still no recognition of the concept of private property. When Kamehameha II died in 1824, the ali'i held onto their land rather than surrendering their land to the new king for redistribution, as had been customary. Kamehameha III was then only twelve years old, and thus power was held by a regent on his behalf Ka'ahumanu.

Although missionaries in Hawai'i were originally, supported by their churches back in New England, their financial support was cut by 1837, during a recession in the United States. Most missionaries and their offspring then decided to stay, and some became more economically self-supporting by embarking on commercial ventures joined by merchants who were moving to the Islands. One such venture was the first major sugarcane plantation, which opened at Kōloa, Kaua'i, in 1835 on land leased by King Kamehameha III. The ali'i, however, would not allow commoners to work on the plantation until the king overruled them (Kuykendall 1938:176). Dissatisfied with conditions of labor, they went on strike in 1841 (Beechert 1992:231), and the enterprise went bankrupt within a decade because the local population was not happy with the requirements of toiling for a capitalist enterprise (Hitch 1992:51).

As the Islands continued to attract small-scale businesses from abroad, chiefs in some cases generously provided gifts of small plots of land to foreign companies. But verbal agreements about the terms of the transfer were unsatisfactorily settled by the kingdom's courts. As a result, foreigners asked consular representatives to threaten to summon warships so that their citizens could prevail in contract disputes.

As transportation costs declined dramatically during the nineteenth century due to better technology in shipbuilding (La Croix 2010:28), the realization emerged among Caucasian entrepreneurs that a lot of money could be made from sugar exports to the United States. Accordingly, many more workers would have to be recruited to clear the land, plant the crops, and harvest the bounty before sales could be made in the continental United States.

But there would be no reserve capital on hand until the first crop, so a bank loan was needed to start up. Accordingly, the capitalists persuaded the government to pass a law in 1841 law allowing the ali'i to lease land to foreigners for up to fifty-five years by means of written contracts. Bankers in the United States were unimpressed, however, requiring transferable assets as collateral. The entrepreneurs, therefore, needed title to the land in order to establish commercially viable plantations, but the local people organized petitions in the 1840s, asking the king not to grant land ownership and naturalization to the Caucasian entrepreneurs (Kealoha-Scullion 1995).

Private property instituted

Caucasian advisers then prevailed on the king to introduce a system of private property. After Kamehameha III consulted with the nobility, which controlled land worked by commoners, he generously agreed to establish the right of private property – not under duress. Capitalists could then obtain large plots of arable land, a sine qua non for capitalist accumulation in agriculture.

Under the terms of the so-called Great Māhele of 1848, the newly established legislature agreed to redistribute land as follows: 39 percent for the ali'i, 24 percent for the crown, 36 percent as government land, and 1 percent for the commoners or maka'āinana (Kent 1983:31; MacKenzie 1991:8). For the ali'i, the redistribution was a windfall. Yet the most productive land was held by the commoners. The rest of the land consisted of forests and mountains that controlled the supply of downstream water (Kuykendall 1938:294). Still, foreigners did not own any land.

In 1850, to implement the Great Māhele, the legislature adopted the Kuleana Act, which enabled Native Hawaiians to file a claim to gain title for their own kuleana (land where they lived and put to productive use). Some 8 percent of the land was then allocated from the ali'i to the maka'āinana, provided they paid hefty fees to survey the land and registered their titles. If they failed to do so, others could file claims of adverse possession. Thus, Native Hawaiians suddenly were allowed their own private property, provided they followed complex legal regulations. Caucasian entrepreneurs then entreated the Native Hawaiians to sell land where they had been living for centuries at profits that must have seemed staggering. By 1852, three dozen foreigners had acquired 219 acres (Lind 1938:55) in advance of the

1855 deadline. As sugarcane plantations were launched, owners seized sources of irrigation water, making traditional farming almost impossible (Kelly 1956:131).

Land sales, of course, enriched the nobility, who allowed the commoners to be dispossessed of their right to live on ancestral land, but commoners were forced to sell their labor in the capitalist market. Accordingly, the grip of the nobility over the commoners was over, as the latter were free to shop for employers, while the former had starting capital for enterprises of their own. Commoners then became tenants on land owned by foreigners, who controlled two-thirds of the land by 1886 (Morgan 1948:137). Displaced Native Hawaiians thenceforth needed to sell their labor in order to feed themselves and pay rent on land where they had once been self-sufficient farmers.

Native Hawaiian commoners at first worked for sugarcane plantation owners, but that work was not very lucrative or rewarding. Some then decided to revert to small-scale agriculture or learn trades. Accustomed to hard work in the precapitalist era, they applied themselves with diligence in the new occupations.

To achieve prosperity, White capitalists needed not only land, but more workers. During the same year as the Kuleana Act, the legislature passed the Masters and Servants Act, similar to indentured servant statutes once adopted in the British Empire. There were not enough Native Hawaiians willing to harvest sugarcane, so recruiters went to China to find laborers, who did so with capitalist expectations, coming in many cases with the desire to send money back home. Under the terms of the law, Chinese and later Japanese workers had to sign three- to five-year contracts before their arrival. Slavery was illegal in Hawai'i, but provisions were so stringent that workers could be jailed and sentenced to hard labor in prison if they failed to show up for work or left the plantation before their contracts expired. Plantation owners tried to keep them on the plantations even after their contracts expired by persuading White businesses to refuse to hire them in the towns.

During the American Civil War (1861–1865), sugar from the Southern states in rebellion was not available to the Northern states, so there was a boom in sugar production in Hawai'i. After the war, the economy plunged. Sugar interests then petitioned Washington to provide duty-free access to the American market. In 1876, Congress ratified the Sugar Reciprocity Treaty, which allowed Hawaiian sugar to be sold without tariff restrictions, thereby giving the kingdom an advantage over other sugar-growing countries. More workers were then imported.

In addition to sugarcane, the Island economy developed exports in rice, coffee, salt, and other commodities (Hitch 1992:44–6). When pineapple was introduced, the selling price was initially so high that consumers believed that the product was a luxury item.

Organization of capitalism

Capitalism has not always been welcomed because monarchs and nobles have felt threatened. The French revolution was far more turbulent, using the guillotine to eliminate the royal class. Capitalism in Hawai'i was embraced as an opportunity by the native people to share abundance despite the more individualistic, selfish form of capitalism brought by Westerners. But capitalism was a challenge, as everyone had to find a source of income.

Bills of exchange were first printed in 1823, the first bank was chartered in 1858 in response to the whaling trade, and coins were minted for the first time in 1883 (ibid.:48). However, the U.S. dollar became the legal tender of the Islands in 1876.

To market agricultural goods and bring in supplies, an agent was needed in the port of Honolulu. As the agents bought enough stock in the planta-tions, they were eventually able to control 96 percent of the plantations that they serviced (Hendricks, Mak, and Tamaribuchi 1989), giving rise to what became known as the "Big Five" firms, which dominated the economy through interlocking directorates, a concentration of economic power far in excess of any area in the United States (Hendricks, Mak, and Tamaribuchi 1989:91–3; Gray 1972:75).

Full-blown capitalism had arrived. The feudal caste system of nobility and commoners was no more. Social classes divided the population. A class struggle gradually emerged in which management held almost all of the power.

Thousands of desertion cases went before the courts by the end of the century to force plantation employees back to work on the plantations; the desertion rate was reported to be 85 percent (Beechert 1985:47–8). The main reason for desertion, according to an industry assessment, was that the recruiters did not pick qualified workers, so selection was more carefully done thereafter (Hitch 1992:70–1).

However, the success of production on a land with a chronic labor short-age meant that unrest would become manifest: workers knew they were indispensable but treated badly. Plantation conditions did not match the promises of labor recruiters. For example, Chinese had to endure crowded living quarters, floggings, docked pay for no apparent reason, and a working day beyond the terms of the labor contract. Chinese Consuls in Honolulu did not come to the aid of workers, and one even provoked the mother of a recalcitrant worker from China to suicide (Budnick 2005:89). Chinese complained, and the Board of Immigration under the Kingdom of Hawai'i was often sympathetic to complaints but only had the power to issue verbal reprimands to plantation owners for mistreatment of workers.

When workers arrived on contract, especially at the prodding of the Japanese government, plantation owners prided themselves on being "paternalistic" (Fuchs 1961:269) by providing housing, recreation, and health care. Nevertheless, there was a series of strikes in the late nineteenth century. Strikes were initially small in scale, peaceful, and well organized. The first strike came in 1867, when dockworkers refused to load a ship until their pay was increased. They struck again in 1868, 1880, 1886, and 1889, eventually joining the International Longshoreman's Association in 1903 (Hitch 1992:129–30). Conservative craft unions, limited to Caucasians, began to form, starting with typographers in 1884 (Hitch 1992:127).

The most intense action was on the plantations, pitting various non-White groups against White managers. In 1891, some 300 Chinese protested in Kohala plantation against a labor recruiter who demanded that they deduct a portion of their wages to pay for the cost of their previous sea passage (PCA 1891). The Chinese believed that no such provision was in their contract. Riots of Chinese workers in 1897 and 1899 were more strident. In the latter case, Japanese laborers offered to assist the police in subduing the Chinese, though the offer was declined.

Some workers returned to China in the period after 1880. Other Chinese married Native Hawaiians and remained in agriculture, engaging primarily in rice farming. Most Chinese, however, left the plantations for the towns to become bakers, butchers, cooks, dressmakers, laundry owners, restaurateurs, storekeepers, street peddlers, and tailors. When they left for town after work contracts, they became capitalists, annoying the Caucasians because of their competitiveness.

Similar to the Chinese, most Japanese arriving in Hawai'i to work on the plantations discovered that conditions were much worse than they had been led to believe (Takaki 1983). Japanese were paid less than Chinese for the same work. Many violated their work contracts by trying to move from one plantation to another in order to escape the whip of cruel overseers (Lind 1938:224). Although many plantation disturbances were reported in the local press during the 1890s, they were minor compared to major strikes after Hawai'i became a Territory of the United States in 1900.

The strikes in Hawai'i were overshadowed by the Haymarket Massacre of 1886, when eleven died, and the Pullman strike of 1894, when thirty were gunned down within the continental United States (Lindsay 1943; Green 2006).

Unlike government resistance to strikes within Europe and the United States during the last half of the nineteenth century, the monarchs allowed strikes, leaving White businesses to settle disputes on their own. The Aloha for capitalism and associated increased prosperity was embraced with enthusiasm during the last half of the nineteenth century.

Hawai'i-style capitalism

Capitalism has not always been welcomed because monarchs and nobles have felt threatened. Capitalism in Hawai'i was embraced as an opportunity by the native people to share abundance despite the more individualistic, selfish form of capitalism brought by Westerners.

Hawai'i subscribed to international free trade at a time when protective tariffs were erected around the world. Even today, many countries are reluctant to accept globalization, as one of the consequences can be movement of immigrants to places lacking Aloha.

8   Foreigners overwhelm natives

Visitors and settlers

History is filled with situations where violence erupts when new peoples try to enter the homelands of others. Based on a true story, the film *Turtle Beach* (1992) depicts Malaysians massacring Vietnamese boat people as they look for somewhere to land, while escaping from the extension of the rule of Ho Chi Minh to the south of the country.

Not so in Hawai'i. The first group of Polynesians to land in the Islands doubtless found conditions quite difficult at first. Later arrivals brought more livestock and vegetables, so there was an expectation that anyone unexpectedly docking in port might possess something special. Spanish visited in the sixteenth century, apparently bringing iron objects (Daws 1968:4), and they returned quietly on several occasions before Captain Cook's arrival.

When the British landed in 1778, they were viewed in a positive light by the Native Hawaiians. Traders in the early nineteenth century reported amazement at how their ships were approached by the indigenous people with friendly faces, warm greetings, and offers of food and water. Although some of the interest was motivated by curiosity over what the foreign crew had on board to be exchanged or purloined, encounters with the Island population were mostly altruistic for the most part, showing Aloha toward newcomers. Native Hawaiians, unlike some indigenous peoples in the Pacific, did not respond with violence against the foreign intruders.

Spanish explorers arriving in the sixteenth century (Fornander 1880:ii, 360) evidently decided not to take up residence. Sailors aboard Captain Cook's ships in the 1770s also returned home. *Haole*, the Hawaiian word for someone who could not speak the Hawaiian language, was applied to Cook and his crew, but the word in time became synonymous with Caucasian or White.

In the 1820s, Caucasian (Haole) missionaries arrived on temporary assignments but decided to settle when they liked what they encountered, though they had less political influence than White traders who arrived from that era (Meller 1958). To obtain menial labor, Caucasian business elites imported persons of several ethnic groups as laborers (Table 8.1).

Table 8.1 Streams of labor immigration to Hawai'i by racial group, 1830–1898

Racial Group	Era of Arrival	Number Arriving	Percentage Male	Percentage Children	Percentage of Total
Mexicans	1830s	200	na	na	.1
Chinese	1852–1885	28,000	89	5	7.0
	1886–1899	28,700	na	na	7.2
South Sea Islanders	1859–1884	2,500	87	11	.6
Portuguese	1878–1886	17,500	57	46	4.4
	1906–1913	5,500	60	43	1.4
Norwegians	1881	600	84	20	.2
Germans	1881–1888, 1897	1,300	72	36	.3
Japanese	1868, 1885–1898	45,000	82	1	11.3
	1898–1907	114,000	82	1	28.6
	1898	370	83	25	.1

Sources: Glick (1980:10); Lind (1980:37; 1982:12); Nordyke (1989:91, 253); Schmitt (1977:25).

Key: na = Figures not available.

Note: "Percentage male" is the ratio of male adults to all adults, children excluded. South Sea Islanders came from the countries now known as Fiji, Kiribati, Papua New Guinea, and Vanuatu.

Early immigrants

The first immigrants were some 200 Mexican vaqueros, who came in the 1820s from San Gabriel Mission because they had experience managing cattle in California. The new Caucasian settlers and whalers had a taste for beef, prompting the establishment of cattle ranches.

The first Chinese peddler appeared in Honolulu during 1823, and some 124 Chinese men were running shops in town by 1853. Chinese showed their loyalty by financing a grand ball for those in power during 1856 (Budnick 2005:179). When males in China were willing to sign contracts for fixed periods of work on the plantations, government officials and plantation owners imagined that the workers would be as gracious as the merchants.

Plantation owners initially sought Native Hawaiians for work in the sugarcane fields. Some were excellent workers, but others did not enjoy the tasks and quit, reverting to traditional agricultural pursuits. In view of the demand for more workers, the king agreed to allow thousands of Chinese to come in the 1850s, when the Taiping Rebellion created considerable uncertainty within China. About 56,000 Chinese arrived as sugarcane plantation workers from 1851 to the mid-1880s (Table 8.1).

But many Chinese quickly left the plantations to farm rice in the rural areas or set up carpentry and cleaning businesses in the towns. When the Civil War in the United States cut off sugar from the Southern to the

Northern states, sugar from Hawai'i was in much greater demand, so more Chinese were recruited. But plantation owners were unpleasantly surprised when the Chinese "coolies," as they were often called, continued the flight to the cities when their work contracts expired or went on strike to protest conditions of work. In response, a so-called Chinese Exclusion Act passed in 1886, stipulating that Chinese would only be admitted if they promised to stay on the plantations, but exemptions under the law permitted importation of an additional 15,000 Chinese during the 1890s (Lind 1938:250).

Plantation owners then decided to achieve greater diversification among their workers in order to avoid having a single ethnic group dominate the labor market, providing the potential for a general strike (Hawai'i 1895: 23–4, 28, 36; Gray 1972:65). The monarchs had no objections to wider recruitment. Many Japanese were recruited from the mid-1880s, as the turmoil of the Meiji Restoration era dispossessed many Japanese who had been accustomed to the security of feudalism.

Few Americans were interested in plantation work in Hawai'i. A few African Americans moved from the continental United States during the nineteenth century and were generally well received in Hawai'i. They were known as Pōpolos, an affectionate nonderogatory term to describe their dark skin. A very few were recruited for plantation work, but they left the fields very quickly for other pursuits, blending into the multiethnic composition of the Territory without incident. The only Caucasian immigrant group of any size was from Portugal.

Immigration Aloha

Despite the kingdom's loopholed Chinese Exclusion Act of 1886, there was little opposition to immigration per se during the nineteenth century. All groups were welcomed by the monarchs and valued by businesses for their role in advancing the sugar industry, which brought prosperity to those not living on the plantations.

Within Hawai'i, several cultural groups adapted to life in the Islands without giving up their own cultures. Few adult Chinese or Japanese spoke English, and they were not offered linguistic schooling. Large numbers were segregated within separate housing enclaves at each plantation. No authority ever asked them to assimilate after their arrival during the nine-teenth century.

In other words, many racial groups coexisted in Hawai'i during the nineteenth century without pressures to assimilate – that is, they were not pressured to abandon their own cultural norms and to adopt new norms of a dominant group. Native Hawaiian monarchs were in power, spread the norms of their own culture by example, and welcomed groups with

Table 8.2 Population of Hawai'i by major racial group, 1778–1900 (horizontal percentages are in parentheses)

Year	Total	Hawaiian	White	Chinese	Japanese
1778	300	**300** (100)			
1853	73	**71** (97)	2 (2)	– (–)	
1860	70	**67** (96)	2 (3)	1 (1)	
1866	63	**59** (93)	2 (4)	2 (2)	
1872	57	**52** (91)	3 (5)	2 (4)	
1878	58	**48** (82)	4 (7)	6 (10)	
1884	81	**44** (55)	17 (21)	18 (23)	– (–)
1890	90	**41** (45)	19 (21)	17 (19)	13 (14)
1896	109	**40** (36)	22 (21)	22 (20)	24 (22)
1900	154	38 (24)	29 (19)	26 (17)	**61** (40)

Sources: Lind (1967:28); Nordyke (1989:178–9, 183).

Key: na = Figures not available.
– = less than 1,000 or less than 1 percent.
(–) = less than 1 percent.

Note: Figures are in 000s. Parenthesized figures are percentages of the civilian and military population, and add to 100 when other ethnic groups are included. For 1778, Stannard (1989) claims 800,000. "Hawaiian" figures include persons with any Native Hawaiian ancestry, though are undercounted (Hoover 2009). "White" figures usually include Portuguese. Figures in boldface identify the highest in each row. Left out of the statistics are those of mixed ancestry.

differing cultural norms, though they were reduced from a majority to a plurality by 1890. Thus, Hawai'i became a multiethnic society harboring persons of many distinct cultural backgrounds and languages toward the end of the nineteenth century (Table 8.2).

A new language emerges

The presence of so many diverse groups living in separate housing communities on the plantations posed an unusual adjustment to diverse children of the laborers. As everywhere, children like to play, and Native Hawaiian children played with immigrant children despite language differences. To communicate, they initially used languages spoken at home mixed with the English that they learned at school. Gradually, the children began to pick up words in languages that were foreign to them. Similar to the Chinese language, the new tongue lacked articles and had many monosyllabic words. What happened was the development of a Creole language. Colloquially known as "pidgin English," but now identified by linguists as a separate language because of a unique syntax, the result was the formation of Hawaiian Creole English (Bickerton 1998).

Meanwhile, immigrant parents were eager to learn English, the language of commerce, but there was no adult school for them. When children went home for dinner after going to school in the morning and playing in the afternoon, they taught their parents the new Creole tongue derived from their peers at play. As a result, two generations of immigrants, along with Native Hawaiians, were speaking a new language that was unintelligible to the White population, which spoke conventional English.

Even after a third immigrant generation learns better English, non-Whites retain bilingual capabilities in the Creole and English languages. Speaking "pidgin" now symbolizes camaraderie among non-Whites in contrast with the Caucasians who discriminated against them (Meredith 1965). Even in the present, almost everyone growing up the Islands learns Hawaiian Creole English, which is fun to speak and is a reminder that Whites can never dominate the Islands again. Those relocating to Hawai'i encounter Creole expressions in everyday life, and will find themselves articulating them to show progress in adapting to the unique Island culture of Aloha.

Conclusion

Thus, the idea of immigration diversity was widely accepted in Hawai'i, even though certain first-generation immigrants suffered discrimination. Rather than rivalry between the various immigrant groups, as was once the case between Irish and Italians on the East Coast of the United States, the immigrant groups in the Islands have built the kind of unity prescribed by the Aloha Spirit. Native Hawaiians have always looked up to their ideals, not down.

Yet resistance to immigration roils the politics of Western Europe and the United States today. Two distinguished scholars have even attacked the growing number of Spanish-speaking immigrants as threats to American culture (Schlesinger 1991; Huntington 2004). The situation in Hawai'i has been very different, a humble acceptance of the desire to preserve a harmonious life and accept newcomers for enriching Island diversity. Nevertheless, a society with many different ethnic groups will have to learn how to live together, and discriminatory practices may emerge, as the next chapter outlines.

9 Differential treatment based on race and sex

Defining "race"

Sometime during the nineteenth century, the idea took hold in Hawai'i that the term *race* was broadly identified with ethnicity and national origin. Caucasians were considered a race differing from Native Hawaiians. Mexicans were so labeled because their ancestry was from México. As workers were imported from countries in Asia, each group was identified by their country of origin. As a result, Chinese, Japanese, Koreans, and others groups from Asia remain separately identified in the Islands and were so counted in the kingdom's census. Despite the later American federal effort to label them as "Asians" for purposes of affirmative action and census categorization, the people of the Islands do not use the term "Asian" to describe those from the different countries with distinct cultures (Okamura 1994). Workers imported from the Azores, though Caucasian, were separately labeled as Portuguese; their initial roles were as plantation supervisors, not the equal of plantation owners. However, the few plantation workers from continental Europe were considered Haoles.

In recent years, the term *Haole* has sometimes been used by Native Hawaiian leaders to refer specifically to the group of Caucasians from Europe and the United States who overthrew the monarchy. A second use of Haole is anyone Caucasian, since the terms *Caucasian* and *White* are almost never used colloquially in the Islands. Another use of the term Haole is to describe Whites from the continental United States who have not absorbed the culture of the Islands, naïvely behaving as they would back home; thereby, they set themselves apart. The phrase *Haole Haole,* with the emphasis on the first word, is now used to describe the latter misfits. In other words, terms referring to ethnic groups and races in Hawai'i are clearly constructed for social convenience (cf. Appiah 2015).

In any case, racial differences were duly noted and even celebrated. In some cases, the distinctions became the basis for discriminatory treatment, although racism (the deliberate subordination of a racial group to have fewer rights) was impossible so long as the monarchs were in power, eager to ensure that Hawai'i remained the land of Aloha. Discrimination was most evident on the plantations, where Whites were in charge.

Employment practices

Under the monarchy's constitution of 1840, imported workers had the same rights as citizens, but jail sentences were meted out to those who refused to honor their work contracts after arrival, and there are reports of whippings of those deemed lazy (Daws 1968:180). In the 1850s, many plantation workers walked off their jobs, turning to other pursuits, but the rest were trapped on islands from which they could not easily escape. Those who went on strike were blackballed for employment on other plantations.

In 1850, the Masters and Servants Act established an indentured servitude similar to laborers brought to North America from Britain during the eighteenth century – in effect, a system of legal peonage. Although in 1867 the sentence was reduced to a fine, desertion was still grounds to extend their work contracts – a provision repealed in 1882 (Conan 1946:56; Fuchs 1961:87). Still, the penal code provided that juries must be of the same race as defendants (Nelligan and Ball 1992) – except for violation of work contracts, where alien Chinese and Japanese would face juries of citizens, who were most likely to be Native Hawaiians and Whites.

After Chinese headed for the towns to set up businesses, their Chinatowns were harassed by the Caucasian media for alleged thievery and filthy living conditions (Fuchs 1961:91–4). There was an outcry in the towns to stop importing Chinese, but plantation owners in rural areas needed cheap labor, and Canton was one place where they could go to replenish their dwindling supply. A Board of Immigration was established in 1864 to regulate the flow. In 1874, the Board of Health restricted some Chinese businesses by requiring a license to sell cakes. Then in 1880, the Board required all pork to be baked in traditional Hawaiian ovens. And in 1891, the Board required the inspection of the sale of all fish and meat. But such regulations, which had more impact on the cost of Chinese businesses, were presumed to improve public health, not driving Chinese out of business, and they complied. Chinese soon formed benevolent and commercial associations to look after their community. But an anti-Chinese movement of Native Hawaiians gained force outside the plantation (Beechert 2011:199), resulting in the mild Chinese exclusion law of 1886.

Japanese were imported to fill the labor shortage from the mid-1880s. Some had entered in 1868 without permission of the Japanese government.

Because they complained about working conditions upon their return home (Burrows 1947), Tokyo was cautious about putting their nationals at risk. Unlike the Chinese, who arrived as individuals, the second flow was on the basis of bilateral treaty signed in 1886. Tokyo carefully regulated the flow, sending labor inspectors to oversee compliance, as the agreement covered standards of pay, health care, housing, and education for their children. Strikes by Japanese workers were often organized when plantation owners did not comply with those standards. Most Japanese were literate and eager for their children to receive a good education, though one third returned to Japan and another third migrated to the continental United States (cf. Coffman 2003:17, 22).

Japanese were attracted to work for $15 per month, then at a level higher than in the home country (Beechert 1985:123; Moriyama 1985:18). But wages were set on the basis of race, with Caucasians paid the most, then Chinese, and Japanese at the bottom of a caste system (Conan 1946). Most supervisory personnel consisted of Native Hawaiians and Portuguese; the rest were Caucasians. Japanese, similar to the Chinese, began to migrate from the plantations to the towns when their work contracts expired, seeking a better life.

Education

All ethnic groups spoke their native languages at home, and schools were no different. But the Hawaiian monarchs were eager to learn English, the language of commerce.

Missionaries learned the Hawaiian language after their arrival and decided to produce a Romanized written version. By 1834, they published the first Hawaiian-language newspapers (Chapin 2011:106). Several books were published in the language – a vocabulary in 1836, a grammar in 1854, and a dictionary in 1865 (Andrews 1865; Elbert and Pukui 1954).

In 1831, meanwhile, the monarchy established Lahaināluna School, the first public school offering secondary education west of the Rocky Mountains. The king was aware of the innovations of Horace Mann, who became the head of the Massachusetts educational system in 1837. Then in 1840, the Privy Council established the Ministry of Education, the third country to do so (after the Polish-Lithuanian Commonwealth in 1773 and France in 1828), and in 1841 Hawai'i became the first country in the world to offer primary education for all children. The goal of universal primary education was declared in 1848, though mandatory attendance was not required in the Islands until later.

Common schools, for nonelite Native Hawaiian children, provided instruction solely in the Hawaiian language up to 1854, when English was introduced. Parents paid $2 per child in the common schools, but $3 per child in *select schools* (Reinecke 1935). *Select schools* were of three types – (1) boarding schools for children of the ali'i (nobility) away from the "corrupting" influence of parents; (2) the O'ahu Charity School for offspring of mixed Native Hawaiian-White parentage, as some were abandoned by seafaring fathers; and (3) various private schools for Caucasians. Tuition was abolished in 1888 for the common (public) schools and in 1896 for private schools. A few Chinese, German, and Portuguese language schools opened in the 1880s, but they were dwarfed by Japanese language schools, which operated out of Buddhist and Shinto missions (Brieske 1961:305–8). In other words, schooling was separated based on race, though without invidious segregation.

The most famous private school, Punahou, opened as a missionary school in 1841. The first English-language private school west of the Mississippi, Punahou demonstrated racial discrimination by initially limiting enrollment to Caucasians. Nevertheless, Native Hawaiians were first allowed to attend in 1848, provided they were "wealthy and civilized" (Pennybacker 1991:121). The earliest Chinese student entered Punahou in 1867, and the first Japanese in 1885 (Forbes 1991:461).

Due to the preference given to Caucasians at Punahou, other private schools, notably 'Iolani and St. Andrew's Priory, began in the last half of the nineteenth century primarily to accommodate Native Hawaiians (in 1863 and 1867, respectively). Since they had no racial quotas, they became multiethnic as soon as Asian parents could afford to send their children to private schools.

In 1887, the first class was enrolled at a new private school, Kamehameha Schools. Students consisted entirely of Native Hawaiians, screened for their academic potential. What had happened to create the endowment for the school is that Princess Bernice Pauahi was heir to all private lands owned by Kamehameha V, the last of the ruling line. When the king died, she inherited the lands. She married banker Charles Bishop, who was accustomed to dealing with land trusts. She then set up a trust, known as the Bishop Estate, so that the lands would be managed by trustees with the stipulation that they would be used for the benefit of Island children, including a school that would enroll Native Hawaiians. An 1884 codicil provided that the land could be leased or sold if "necessary for the establishment and maintenance of said schools, or for the best interests of the estate" (Sullam 1976:4–5). Because Kamehameha Schools is not a public school, the enrollment preference for Native Hawaiians was not considered to be an example of racism, since the government was not involved in subordinating anyone. However, the initial trustees were Caucasians, who insisted that English be the sole medium of instruction, and the instructors were not Native Hawaiians. The school's administrators assumed that Native Hawaiians were intellectually deficient, so the kingdom's public schools actually offered a better education (Glick 1980:300–1).

Mistreatment of women

Although Queen Kaʻahumanu acted as premier and later Queen Liliʻuokalani played a prominent role politically, the missionaries brought with them the common law practice of coverture – that is, Caucasian women lost all civil rights as soon as they married; they were legally subordinate to their husbands. Caucasian control over the legal system meant the imposition of coverture on married Native Hawaiian women, whose right to enter into contracts was specifically denied by a law passed in 1846 (Asato 1981).

No such practice existed before the missionaries (Gething 1977). Women were not barred from voting according to the 1840 constitution. But women lost the right to vote in the 1852 constitution.

Meanwhile, women working at the same jobs as men received less pay (Takaki 2008:240). On the plantations, where they were 14 percent of the workforce, women were assigned to cutting cane, hoeing, stripping leaves, and harvesting.

Voting

The kingdom's first constitution, adopted in 1840, allowed universal adult suffrage; women were not excluded. However, women lost the right to vote in the 1852 constitution.

As the economic influence of Caucasian citizens grew, Native Hawaiians engaged in bloc voting on election days (Daws 1968:213). But so did Caucasians, who influenced adoption of a new constitution in 1864 that limited the franchise to those with literacy and a minimum amount of income or property, requirements later abolished by the constitution of 1874.

However, the wealth qualification was reinstituted in the constitution of 1887, which transferred most power from the monarch to the legislature; two-thirds of the Native Hawaiians were no longer qualified to vote (Daws 1968:242). The new restrictions had the deliberate effect of giving more power to Caucasians and taking power from Native Hawaiians. Whereas the 1864 constitution could be characterized as institutionalizing discrimination, the 1887 document was clearly racist, guaranteeing the vote to "residents" of the Islands who met the qualifications. In other words, Caucasians who had not become citizens of Hawaiʻi could now exercise the franchise, whereas the Supreme Court interpreted the "residency" clause to disallow even naturalized Chinese citizens of Hawai'i from voting (Glick 1980:224). The shift in political power in the 1887 constitution was because a coup in effect had occurred.

Conclusion

Mistreatment based on race was mostly a Caucasian idea, whether in employment, education, voting, or restrictions imposed on women. Such racism usually sews the seeds of ethnic unrest, as in the Jim Crow era of the American south. Yet most Native Hawaiians were not concerned as long as the monarchy was still in power, and as long as they constituted a majority of the population.

10 Civil unrest and coup attempts

Early coup attempts

Efforts to displace rulers occurred from time to time before the arrival of Captain Cook (Fornander 1880). When a chief died, ownership over his geographic domain was often settled in battle (Daws 1968:72).

Thus, some discontent about ruler succession surfaced on one occasion after Kamehameha unified the islands. In 1824, Kaumuali'i, the former ruler of Kaua'i, died on O'ahu. He had been taken virtual prisoner in 1821 by Kamehameha II, who took over his domain on Kaua'i. But Kaumuali'i's son George would not accept his disinheritance and attacked the fort at Waimea, Kaua'i. Troops were then sent by Kamehameha II to put down the rebellion, which was crushed in 1825.

Visiting sailors engage in race riots

In 1826, a near race riot erupted. American sailors docking in port were eager to have sex with women. But Hiram Bingham, unofficial leader of the missionaries, had persuaded the king to ban prostitution. After two months, the sailors could not stand their abstinence anymore, so they went to protest at Bingham's church and broke windows during a Sunday service. Bingham tried to escape, but when they chased after him, some Native Hawaiians accepted the challenge and beat back the sailors. Nevertheless, O'ahu Governor Boki soon relaxed the ban, and they were able to quench their lasciviousness.

A similar riot broke out, pitting sailors against locals, in 1852. This time the pretext was the death of a sailor in jail who had been arrested for drunkenness. The warden heard him throwing rocks at the prison door, went into his cell in the dark, and clubbed him. Learning that he was dead, his fellow comrades then rioted, seeking to lynch the warden: they surrounded and then entered the police station and set the police station and other buildings on fire. When firefighters arrived, the White mob cut their hoses. They invaded grog shops, emptying their liquor supplies, and set forth to attack homes of government ministers. The following morning the Marshall of the Kingdom declared martial law, and a militia of 250 cleared the streets.

Annexation talk

Despite the two inconsequential "White riots," in 1853, the kingdom considerably thinned down its army, which was bankrupting the treasury (ibid.:138, 205). During that year, White residents favoring annexation by the United States launched a propaganda war, so a draft treaty of cession was drawn up. They hoped to bully the government into signing. American warships were in port, and some weapons were suspiciously unloaded. A government militia was mobilized at the waterfront in case hostile soldiers were to disembark. But nothing happened.

Talk shifted in 1854 to the idea of a reciprocity treaty that would eliminate tariffs in bilateral trade with the United States, but to no avail. Although such a treaty was finally accepted by the monarchy in 1867, the U.S. Senate would not ratify the document, and the pro-annexationists dropped the campaign for the time being. Nevertheless, the United States began a permanent rotation of warships from that year (Ferguson and Turnbull 2010).

End-of-the-world prophesy

Government force was used to quell a weird civil disturbance in 1868. One-time legislator and judge, Kaona imagined that the world was soon ending and that only a strip of land in South Kona would be spared. He and his followers then occupied the land and refused to leave. The local sheriff sent a posse, a scuffle ensued, and the sheriff mobilized a biracial force that arrested the group.

Election bribery

When King Kamehameha V died in 1872, he had no male heir, and he had not officially designated a successor. The country's constitution gave the power to name a successor to the legislature, which held an election for that purpose in 1873. The two most popular candidates were Prince William Lunalilo and David Kalākaua, who had lesser royal blood. Lunalilo won, but because White commercial interests bribed voters, the outcome was the equivalent of a coup.

Opposition to loss of sovereignty

Hawai'i's boom in sugar exports during the American Civil War ended when production resumed in Louisiana after the North defeated the South, resulting in a serious economic downturn. Talk about a reciprocity treaty that would grant duty-free access to bilateral trade emerged. But many Native Hawaiians were opposed on hearing rumors about the possibility of ceding Pearl Harbor to the United States as part of the deal, and in 1872, King Lunalilo refused to sign a treaty drafted for him by Caucasian advisers.

One day in 1873, some thirty members of the Royal Household Troops mutinied, showing opposition to the prospect of ceding land to another country, and they refused to pay attention to orders from civilian authorities. Public support soon doubled their ranks to about sixty protesters. The ailing king twice tried to quell the uprising, but the mutineers insisted on several demands. After agreeing to their demands, the king disbanded the unit, and the incident was over in six days.

Queen Emma's coup attempt

King Lunalilo died after 13 months in office, so there was another election in 1874. Queen Emma, spouse of Kamehameha V, then indicated that King Lunalilo informally told her that she was next in line. However, the legislature rejected her claim and held an election instead. In the campaign, Emma ran against David Kalākaua, who won. Disgruntled supporters of Emma then entered the legislature, fought supporters of Kalākaua, and vandalized government offices.

The disturbance was so intense that the Caucasian foreign minister invited about 150 American and British troops from warships in port to quell the riot. Marines quickly cleared the chamber and occupied the government building until Emma urged her supporters to support the new king. American gunboats continued to be rotated so as to be available in case of future unrest.

The stage was now set for a revised Reciprocity Treaty, which was ratified in 1875. The United States was allowed to ship several tariff-free goods to the Islands, which could in turn export sugar duty-free. Hawai'i also promised not to conclude a reciprocity treaty with any other country, and not to alienate any land to any other country. The treaty was for a seven-year period and was extended thereafter one year at a time.

The Bayonet Constitution

After 1875, King Kalākaua became increasingly bold in the exercise of power, for example staffing the civil service with sycophants and placing his nobility buddies into the legislature. His spending was bringing the kingdom to the verge of bankruptcy, and he was not getting along with the sugar planters, who controlled the economy.

A group of former military officers formed the Hawaiian Rifles organiza-tion in 1884 with approval of the king. Volney Ashford led the group, which appeared to be a sort of American Legion-type of social group. But White opponents of the monarchy then secretly infiltrated the Hawaiian Rifles.

In 1886, negotiations were underway for an extension and revision of the Reciprocity Treaty, including a provision that would give the U.S. Navy exclusive access to Pearl Harbor. When the king refused to sign the treaty because that provision would involve loss of sovereignty, many Native Hawaiians protested. A plot was then hatched to limit his power.

When rumors spread in 1887 that the government might be overpowered by American troops on board a ship in port, the king called up the Hawai-ian Rifles for protection. But that put him at the mercy of some of his real opponents, who demanded that he sign a new constitution. Now known as the Bayonet Constitution, the constitution made the king into a figurehead without power, and established property ownership requirements for voting, thereby disfranchising all but the middle and upper classes. Even Chinese who had acquired Hawaiian citizenship were disfranchised.

Subsequently that year, the revised Reciprocity Treaty was ratified, allowing the United States to build a "coaling and repair station" – that is, to establish a naval base, at Pearl Harbor. The agreement did not cede any territory, as President Grover Cleveland assured (Kuykendall 1967:396), and nothing much was done to implement the military provisions.

Wilcox revolt

In 1889, part-Hawaiian Robert Wilcox led about seventy-five armed Native Hawaiians in an attempt to take over the government. Their aim was to force King Kālakaua to rescind the constitution that he had signed under duress two years earlier.

After fighting their way to the palace grounds, government forces over-powered them, using munitions acquired from the USS *Adams*, which sent 100 men to quell the uprising. Shots were fired, seven of Wilcox's group died, and they were rounded up. From that point on, American soldiers were in principle available to the government in case of trouble.

Queen Liliʻuokalani's reign

On the death of Kālakaua in 1891, Lydia Kamakaʻeha Paki Liliʻuokalani became queen because Kālakaua had previously designated her as the heir apparent. In 1892, Ashford and others who disapproved of the Bayonet Constitution joined forces with Wilcox. But spies found out, and a false rumor about an impending coup led the government to put sandbags around

'Iolani Palace. However, no coup was in fact being planned, so the incident is sometimes known as the Burlesque Conspiracy.

Queen Lili'uokalani appointed Native Hawaiians to government positions formerly held by Caucasians and made proposals for two revenue innovations that infuriated the missionary descendants – a lottery and the licensing of Chinese opium clubs. Native Hawaiians were so alienated that they felt driven to despair, drunkenness, and suicide, so she wanted to restore her people to a place of dignity. In 1893, she indicated interest in a petition signed by two-thirds of the registered voters to change the constitution to restore some regal power – that is, to void the Bayonet Constitution (McGregor 1991:14). She even drew up a new constitution in secret (Daws 1968:271). When Caucasian members of her Cabinet objected, believing that she was plotting a palace coup, she demurred. But that did not satisfy her opponents. In 1893, a real coup d'état toppled the Kingdom of Hawai'i. The kingdom that had practiced Aloha to enrich the lives of everyone was no more.

Conclusion

The kingdom's only racial unrest was provoked by Whites. Hawai'i was the last major archipelago to lose sovereignty in the Pacific. The anticolonial movement that arose after World War II served as the impetus for the Islands to become the fiftieth state of the United States. But many Native Hawaiians objected that Washington never allowed them the option of voting to regain sovereignty.

Part III

A kingdom falls

Ever since Caucasians entered Hawai'i, there were signs that the peaceful Native Hawaiians would eventually lose their sovereignty. Captain James Cook brought enough firearms to do the job, and colonial powers even threatened to do so. Diseases that became epidemics gradually reduced the size of the population of Native Hawaiians to minority status. The rise of the capitalist plantation economy so undermined self-sufficient agriculture that the indigenous population had to sell its labor to outsiders. Discrimination based on race and sex, contrary to the norms of the Aloha Spirit, could only be transformed into racism – government-imposed subordination of the local population by foreigners – by a coup that would transfer power away from Native Hawaiians. Attempted coups ultimately became better organized. The story of the coup d'état that ended the monarchy is told next.

11 A coup topples a kingdom

The coup

Due to the increasing nationalism exhibited by Queen Lili'uokalani, a secret Annexation Club was formed in 1892, when elections produced a situation in which no political party had a majority. Soon, the club morphed into a secret Committee of Safety, composed of thirteen Caucasians, including five Americans, six White citizens of Hawai'i, a Brit, and a German. Twelve of the thirteen had been members of the Annexation Club. Most were missionary descendants (Fuchs 1961:33). They solicited and gained support from American Consul John Stevens and the captain of the USS *Boston* for a coup but actually never asked them to land; they first wanted to draw up documents for a provisional government.

On January 16, 1893, Stevens unilaterally ordered 162 troops to disembark from the USS *Boston*, seize the government building, place the queen under house arrest, and demand that she abrogate. One palace guard was wounded in the leg of the otherwise peaceful takeover. The monarchs lacked a militia to put down the insurrection.

Instead of conceding power to the conspirators, however, the queen relinquished power to the United States (Lili'uokalani 1898:chs40–7), expecting yet another disavowal, as the British had done in 1842. But none came, and the American flag went up in Honolulu on February 1, when a declaration of a Provisional Government and martial law was announced. President Benjamin Harrison forwarded a treaty of cession to the Senate, which was not then in session. The queen's son, Prince Jonah Kūhiō Kalaniana'ole Pi'ikoi, was soon arrested for advocating her restoration to the throne.

After Grover Cleveland was sworn in as president the following month, he withdrew the treaty from the United States Senate and sent an envoy, James Blount, to Honolulu for an investigation. Based on the resulting report (Blount 1893), which found that most Island residents opposed the coup, Cleveland ordered the flag lowered, the return of American soldiers to their ships, and the withdrawal of the USS *Boston*.

Cleveland characterized the coup as unconstitutional and a violation of international law (Dudley and Agard 1990:25–46): The landing of American troops for the coup violated the Reciprocity Treaty (Dougherty 1992:169), an offense that was an international crime established by the Congress of Vienna in 1815. His Secretary of State, Walter Gresham, even urged him to send American troops to overthrow the upstart regime and to restore the monarchy, but Cleveland instead asked the Provisional Government to restore the monarchy (Daws 1968:278–9; Morgan 2011). Under his administration, the McKinley Tariff of 1890, which placed restrictions on Island sugar contrary to the Reciprocity Treaty, was repealed in 1894. But that did not stop those who wanted annexation.

The Republic of Hawai'i

On July 4, 1894, the coup leaders proclaimed the Republic of Hawai'i, hoping for the eventual election of a different American president. Nevertheless, Cleveland recognized the new government diplomatically to keep the consulate in contact. The next American election was in 1896, when Cleveland was hoping to be re-elected. The next American election was in 1896.

Robert Wilcox mobilized forces in 1895 to bring down the government and restore the monarchy, but his coup failed after ten days. His forces were outmaneuvered in areas outside Honolulu without a shot.

To prevent loss of life, Lili'uokalani decided to abdicate in 1896, whereupon she was released from confinement in the palace to live in the nearby royal residence. She then went to Washington to lobby against annexation by the United States. Fearing annexation, Native Hawaiians organized a petition drive to present to Congress. From 1897–1898, they collected 30,000 signatures (Kauanui 2014:322; Silva 2014).

The Republic evidently feared the "Yellow Peril", as Japan had defeated China in 1895 to gain control over Korea and annexed Taiwan after signing a bilateral peace treaty. In 1897, the Republic of Hawai'i refused the landing of three boatloads of Japanese workers for the plantations in the port of Honolulu, as had been previously arranged by Tokyo. In response, the Japanese government sent three warships to the port of Honolulu with two demands: (1) that the United States should agree not to annex Hawai'i, and (2) that the dispute should be arbitrated, with Washington as the neutral arbitrator. President William McKinley refused both demands. Instead, the Republic of Hawai'i agreed to pay $75,000 in reparations for the incident, and all three Japanese ships sailed home (Morgan 2011).

In 1896, William McKinley was elected and due to take office in 1897. Republic officials went to Washington to lobby for annexation.

Some Caucasians were fearful that Japanese workers, who had been arriving in droves from the 1880s to work the sugarcane fields, formed an underground force plotting to take over the Islands. That thought provoked more interest in having Hawai'i a part of the United States (Coffman 2003:8, 21).

Japan's aggressiveness vis-à-vis China in 1895 and the incident over the Republic's refusal to allow Japanese workers to disembark in Honolulu during 1897 were fresh in the minds of the members of Congress in 1898, but there were insufficient votes in the Senate to ratify the treaty of annexation approved by the Republic. Meanwhile, the American takeover of the Philippines in the Spanish-American War of 1898 melted some opposition to American annexation of the Hawaiian Islands (Russ 1959,1961). But without enough votes for ratification of the treaty, annexation could not proceed.

Annexation

Then an idea emerged to bypass international legal custom and instead have a vote on annexation by both houses of Congress. After all, American military forces were unopposed in the Islands. Accordingly, annexation was approved by majority votes in both the House of Representatives and the Senate that year on the basis of a resolution, not a treaty. The aim was largely strategic, as plantation executives feared that annexation would mean an end to the Masters and Servants Act, which guaranteed them cheap labor (Daws 1968:33).

From 1898, American naval personnel and ships took advantage of the opportunity to occupy Pearl Harbor (Hitch 1992:123). The first permanent military garrison soon arrived. Pearl Harbor Naval Base was established in 1900 but was not dredged to accommodate large vessels until 1908. No further efforts to restore the monarchy could be launched militarily. In 1900, Congress clarified the status of the Islands by adopting the Organic Act, which established the Territory of Hawai'i, similar to other territories that later became states, notably Arizona and New Mexico.

Conclusion

For the first time, Hawai'i had become a colony of another country. Annexation clearly was not in accord with international treaty law. What really happened is that the American military, already stationed at Pearl Harbor, in effect ensured the annexation. Ever since, efforts of the Native Hawaiian people to reverse the annexation have continued off and on, but they have remained patient in seeking redress.

Although plebiscites were held before redrawing the map of Europe after World War I, no vote was ever held to determine their wishes, even when a vote on statehood was called in 1959. Many Native Hawaiians want to return to the halcyon days of the monarchy, as White rule was clearly racist.

12 White racism takes over

Not all Caucasians supported the coup. White royalists were expelled soon after the coup, and plantation owners feared that annexation would deprive them of cheap labor. The conspirators were largely White government officials and their friends, who opposed the repeal of the 1887 Bayonet Constitution. Those supporting the coup were clearly White racists who looked down upon Chinese, Japanese, and Native Hawaiians.

As soon as the Honolulu Whites were in control of the Islands, they instituted changes that adversely affected non-Whites, rolling back the Aloha practiced by the monarchs. The Provisional Government imposed martial law, though they did so after American troops were already in Honolulu, and royalists were hunted down, and 191 were arrested and convicted, including the queen' son (Daws 1968:283), although all were released and pardoned by 1896 (Fuchs 1961:35). Aside from establishing a police state, especially after the abortive Wilcox Revolt of 1895, the takeover mainly affected constitutional, economic, and educational changes.

Constitutional racism

After President Grover Cleveland refused to allow annexation in 1893, the Republic of Hawai'i was proclaimed in 1894, including a constitution similar to the Bayonet Constitution. Property qualifications were raised even more, the minimum voting age was increased from twenty to twenty-one, and voters had to declare allegiance to the Republic and be literate in English. As a result, the voting strength of Native Hawaiians was reduced to only 20 percent of the electorate. Chinese and Japanese born in the Islands were still stripped of voting rights (Daws 1968:281). The Japanese government's demand that its dual citizen emigrants be granted the right to vote was also ignored (Coffman 2003:272). When the election was held later that year, only eighteen delegates were chosen; nineteen were selected by members of the Provisional Government.

The new legislature, in turn, appointed the president of the republic. The right of jury trial was confined to major offenses. A poll tax was imposed in 1896. But the document was an interim measure until anticipated annexation. The government consisted of Caucasians exclusively.

Economic racism

Crown lands, formerly the possession of the monarchs, were declared by the Republic of Hawai'i in 1894 to be government lands. As a result, much of the property could be leased or sold to plantation owners. However, a land act in 1895 limited sales to 1,000 acres and limited leases to twenty-one years (Daws 1961:33).

Due to the serious shortage of plantation workers after the boom created by the repeal of the McKinley Tariff in 1894, the Republic allowed the importation of more Japanese, provided that recruiters promised to bring 10 percent of the new laborers from Europe or the United States. However, they could not meet the new quota.

The Republic of Hawai'i proceeded to crack down on workers, restricting them to work on the plantations under threat of deportation. In 1895, plantation owners formed the Hawaiian Sugar Planters' Association to forge a common policy toward the workers.

In 1897, workers reacted to a cruel overseer at Lihue plantation on Kaua'i in a riot resulted in one death, fifteen deportations, and finally the discharge of the overseer (Fuchs 1961:89–90). That same year, a strike involving about 100 workers arose at Ewa plantation on O'ahu after an overseer broke a worker's arm, whereupon 81 strikers were arrested and jailed as they tried to march to the Japanese Consul to protest (PCA 1897).

In early 1899, some 130 Chinese marched from Spreckelsville toward Wailuku, Maui, to demand reinstitution of hot meals and the release of a fellow worker who had been jailed for assaulting an overseer (Honolulu Independent 1899; PCA 1899c). Later in the year, a riot involving about 100 workers at Wai'anae plantation followed an assault on a Chinese overseer; arrest of the perpetrator resulted in the injury of seventeen and the jailing of four Chinese (PCA 1899a,b). The incidents, minor compared to what happened in the twentieth century, made Chinese determined to get off the plantations, even though they were paid more than Japanese (but less than Portuguese) for the same work.

Racism in education

In 1896, three years after the monarchy was replaced by the Republic of Hawai'i, all children aged six to fifteen were required to go to school,

public or private. All public instruction had to be in English. The requirement pushed aside the Hawaiian language that the missionaries had not only
learned, but also transliterated into Roman text so that for the first time
Hawaiian was a written language. Only three Hawaiian language schools
then existed, and they were required to teach English. Speaking Hawaiian
in public even resulted in beatings (Nakaso 2008). Caucasians running the
Republic boasted that they had created a "linguistic revolution" (Hawai'i
1896:22). Meanwhile, at private Punahou, a ceiling of 10 percent was set
for Asian enrollment in 1896.

The pressure for "Americanization" came after the United States annexed
the Islands in 1898, but consisted mainly of trying to make English (often
spoken with the New England accent brought by the missionaries) the dominant language of economics, politics, and public education.

Chinatowns burn

In 1899, a possibly more subtle form of racism emerged in response to an
outbreak of bubonic plague in the Chinatowns of Maui and O'ahu, where
Republic authorities failed to maintain proper standards of sanitation.
Rather than a quarantine of those afflicted, as usual, the Board of Health
burned affected houses. In 1900, fires got out of control, and most of the
two Chinatowns burned to the ground. Although some were suspicious that
the fire was an anti-Chinese act, there were more Japanese than Chinese
residents in Honolulu's Chinatown (Honolulu Japanese Chamber of Commerce 1970:47).

Evidence of racism emerged after the fire was over: Caucasian businesses
expanded from nearby downtown Honolulu into the areas that had been
burned rather than restoring the area to the original inhabitants. Claims of
$3 million for damages were authorized in 1903, though only $1.3 million
were paid (Budnick 2005:18).

Conclusion

Native Hawaiian rulers actively sought advice from the early Caucasian
settlers, who embraced the Aloha Spirit during the early nineteenth century
(Wooden 1981:22). Later, Whites joined the Cabinets and were elected to
the kingdom's legislature. In effect, there was biracial rule during the last
half of the nineteenth century.

What occurred in 1893 was a phenomenon known as "ethnic displacement" –
that is, the replacement of ruling elites of one ethnic group by elites of
another ethnic group (Eisinger 1980). Native Hawaiians lost power. Haoles,
once identified as White foreigners, became the new rulers, though less

numerous than Native Hawaiians. White racism continued during the era of the Territory of Hawai'i, which lasted from 1900 to 1959. Only after Congress granted statehood to Hawai'i in 1959, with non-Whites still a majority in the population, could the arduous task begin to undo the effects of White racism. But that is the subject for another volume.

Wherever ethnic displacement has occurred elsewhere around the world, whether from colonial rule or mass migration, tensions have often boiled over into violence. Not so in Hawai'i. Colonization of the Islands by the United States, unseating Native Hawaiians in their own land, has created a source of tension that remains as an unresolved conflict on today's political agenda. Nevertheless, Native Hawaiians will remain steadfast in the effort to recapture the glory of a kingdom based on the Spirit of Aloha.

Part IV

Legacy of the Kingdom of Hawai'i

There is a lot to learn from the history of Hawai'i before the Islands became absorbed into the United States of America. In the final chapters, those lessons are spelled out. Chapter 13 identifies the enthusiasm of the kingdom to achieve progress, even leading the world. The aim of Chapter 14 is to communicate to the rest of the world what they could do to perfect race relations, based on the Hawai'i example.

There is another reason for the review: since Hawai'i was annexed contrary to the norms of international law, the day may come when independence and the kingdom may be restored. It is useful to consider what would be reconstituted in that eventuality.

13 Zeal for progress

Aloha for constructive new ideas typifies Hawai'i. There has always been a practical response to the many challenges confronting Hawai'i over the years. The present chapter demonstrates the extraordinary progress of the Islands from the first arrival of the Polynesians to the end of the nineteenth century, when social progress came to a halt with the imposition of alien rule over the Islands. In a word, there has been a fervent quest for progress, well captured by the word *zeal.*

Clearly, the arrival of Captain Cook and various commercial trading ships posed an immediate major challenge. The Islands had little knowledge of the sophistication and technology of the foreigners. The choice was either to be content with the traditional life and possibly lose sovereignty by colonization or modernize and impress the world. Kamehameha and his descendants chose the latter strategy. Kamehameha was so dazzled by the foreigners that he embraced advisers from Britain, Spain, and the United States. He even appointed John Young, boatswain of the English ship *Eleanora*, as governor of his home island from 1802 to 1812, while he was busy on other islands.

If *progress* is defined as keeping up to date with the latest developments and even innovating beyond, then Hawai'i may be characterized as experiencing an almost overnight full-throttled shift from traditional to modern society during the mid-nineteenth century. Those who today depict Islanders as entirely living a life of grass skirts, hula, and ukuleles under gently swaying palm trees spread a stereotype entirely out of sync with the determination and enthusiasm with which those living in Hawai'i have kept pace with and often have soared ahead of the rest of the world since the eighteenth century in matters of navigation, military technology, politics, family life, economics, the environment, historic preservation, and education.

Navigational progress

Economist Thomas Hitch (1992:4–8) has expressed amazement that Native Hawaiians originally traveled thousands of miles to reach the Islands from the Marquesas without a compass or sextant, similar to the feats of astronauts, and were able to carve canoes with stone tools, while developing complex irrigation systems. There is solid evidence that they arrived in North America – California – before Columbus and brought back sweet potatoes from South America, where hotel lodging in Chile is still called *alojamiento*.

Military progress

When Captain Cook arrived, his crew displayed firearms never seen before in the Islands. Native Hawaiians tried to trade or steal whatever they could get. Because a civil war was ongoing, the effect was an arms race around the Islands. Fur traders sailing to and from Canada made easy sales of firearms, but often they sold inoperable weapons. Then came a breakthrough: Kamehameha's allies managed to seize a schooner with all its modern weapons of warfare, thereby ensuring his eventual victory in the ongoing civil war. Because Kamehameha's reign was humane, the civil war ended without lingering bitterness.

In 1816, Kamehameha confronted Russian efforts to build a fort in Honolulu, whereupon they withdrew. He then completed the fortification, which was torn down during the twentieth century.

The supply of arms in the Islands was never a match for warships with well-trained soldiers. The revision of the Reciprocity Treaty in 1887, which allowed the American Navy to enter and develop Pearl Harbor, was an effort to acquire the benefits of modern military defense of the Islands to deter potential German colonization, which was occurring in Samoa and elsewhere in the Pacific, without incurring the costs. The Americans had promised to respect the sovereignty of the monarchy as far back as 1843, so Native Hawaiians were not expecting to be double-crossed in 1893 or 1898.

Constitutional progress

Rule originally operated on the basis of an elaborate series of strict kapus in the context of a feudal economy. They provided a legal framework, though unwritten (Kanahele 1986:44–5).

When Kamehameha assumed control of most of the Islands in 1782, he ruled though a Council of Chiefs and appointed governors for the major islands. He allowed his wife to assume the position of kuhina-nui, a position similar to premier, so that he would have outreach to the people.

Upon the death of Kamehameha the Great in 1819, Kamehameha II became king. One of Kamehameha's wives, whom Kamehameha I had designated as the official guardian of the heir to the throne, Queen Ka'ahumanu, was already at the seat of royal authority, wearing the royal red cape, when she greeted the new king with the words "We shall rule together." She later clarified her role as kuhina-nui (executive officer). One of her first acts was to have the king abolish the kapu system. Her reason was to acquire power, as there had long been a kapu against women assuming political authority. With the abolition of the kapu system, women throughout the Islands could participate in political decision making at the local level and sell their labor in the marketplace. She was one of the world's first successful feminists, having broken through economic and political glass ceilings for all women in the Islands. Now political authority was "no longer guaranteed by the gods" (Daws 1968:57).

Kamehameha II took control in 1819, with Ka'ahumanu serving in effect as premier. He visited London during 1824 in order to meet the royal family and achieve recognition for the modernizing kingdom. However, he died there. Kamehameha III took the throne in 1824, with Ka'ahumanu still serving as premier until her death in 1832, whereupon Elizabeth Kīna'u became the new kuhina-nui in a succession that continued until the position was abolished in 1864.

Although Kamehameha the Great established the capital of the Kingdom of Hawai'i on the island where he was born, with an interval on O'ahu from 1804 to 1812, his sons gravitated toward the centers of trade. In 1820, Kamehameha II moved the capital to Lahainā, the port carrying the bulk of the sandalwood and whaling trade. In 1830, the kingdom was the first country in the world to abolish the death penalty, which was reinstituted when Hawai'i became a Territory of the United States. As the economy of O'ahu boomed, Kamehameha III relocated the capital to Honolulu in 1845. 'Iolani Palace was not constructed until 1882.

Abolition of the kapu system and the arrival of capitalists eager to do business under rule by law prompted the monarchs to adopt a British-style government system with legislative and judicial branches.

In 1839, Kamehameha III issued a Declaration of Rights and the Edict of Toleration. The Rights protected for "all people of all lands" were identified as "life, limb, liberty, freedom from oppression; the earnings of his hands and the productions of his minds." The chiefs were explicitly informed that they would lose their noble status if they mistreated commoners. The Edict immediately allowed the Catholic Church to operate freely, and religious liberty has been observed ever since.

In 1840, on behalf of the "Hawaiian Islands," Kamehameha III and Queen Kekāuluohi promulgated a British-style government. Reference to the "Sandwich Islands" then ceased (Clement 1980). The body of chiefs that formerly met at the pleasure of the king became an appointive sixteen-member House of Nobles, including the king as a member, along with a "representative body," initially chosen by the king from letters of nomination; those with the most nominations were appointed by the king (Kuykendall 1938:228). Calling attention to the power once wielded by Ka'ahumanu, the king appointed a premier to play a similar role vis-à-vis the king.

Any laws required majority support in the two legislative bodies, chosen biennially, as well as approval by the premier and the monarch. All adults in the kingdom were given the power to vote in elections for the representative body. Hawai'i, thus, was the first country to grant women the franchise and the third country (after France and Greece) to grant universal manhood suffrage.

The king also formalized the position of governor for the four main island groups, similar to the present counties. The nobles on each island were empowered to appoint the governors, who would collect taxes on behalf of the king, appoint judges, and have control over military installations in their islands. Judges were to preside in each gubernatorial jurisdiction. There was a right of appeal to the Supreme Court, with the king at the head. Thus, the Kingdom of Hawai'i established rule of law, which provided security to commercial transactions in a manner that even today cannot be ensured in many parts of the world.

Both the Declaration and the Edict were incorporated into the constitution. The right to a fair trial was also included, evidently modeled on the wording of the Sixth Amendment to the American constitution. The constitution also provided that the next monarch, should the king die without an immediate heir, would be decided by a vote of the chiefs or the legislature.

The constitution would not be considered adopted until the provisions were explained to the people, and the persons who were to serve in the government also had to agree to uphold the provisions. Amendments were to be discussed first with the public and then adopted by a majority vote of both legislative chambers.

According to the 1840 constitution, all land was owned by the monarchy on behalf of the chiefs and the people "in common," with the monarch as the protector of the land arrangement, though he could designate crown lands as his own property. But, as mentioned above, the major piece of legislation during the 1840s, the so-called Great Māhele of 1848, established the concept of private property.

In addition, several "gathering rights" were recognized by the Kuleana Act of 1850: those on ancestral agricultural lands to which they claimed title were granted a right of access, even over private land, to gather aho cord, drinking water, firewood, house timbers, running water, thatch, and ti plants (Eagar 1997). During the same year, the legislature designed a criminal code, and secret ballots were adopted.

In 1851, the legislature proposed a three-person commission, with one member appointed by the king and each of the two legislative chambers, to make recommendations to the king for a revised constitution. In 1852, based on the work of the commission, Kamehameha III adopted a more detailed constitution: taxpaying citizens at least twenty years old were enfranchised, whether they owned property or not, but women lost the right to vote. The first articles expanded civil liberties to include all those enumerated in the American Bill of Rights. Slavery, which never existed in the Islands, was prohibited, joining the earlier abolition by France and Scandinavian countries. The king and House of Nobles were given the power to designate a successor to the throne; but if they failed to do so, that power would be exercised jointly by the two legislative bodies.

The position of kuhina-nui was re-established in the 1852 constitution as an executive officer second only to the king, institutionalizing the role once played by Queen Ka'ahumanu. The constitution also provided for a Cabinet Council, consisting of department heads appointed by the monarch. Three-fourths of the Cabinets over the years turned out to be Caucasians (Fuchs 1961:14). There was also a Privy Council, which included the Cabinet, the four island governors, and others appointed by the monarch. The representative body, officially called the House of Representatives, was allowed to have from twenty-four to forty members and had to originate all appropriation legislation. The House of Nobles was to consist of no more than thirty members, appointed by the monarch for life (instead of hereditary roles). The king gave up his role in the Supreme Court, whose members were appointed by the Privy Council and approved by the king. Tribunals under the jurisdiction of the governors became district courts. Adoption of amendments was raised to a two-thirds vote in both houses of the legislature as well as approval by the king, who retained the power to abrogate the constitution.

Nevertheless, Whites continued to seek more power in the government by rolling back democratic progress. After the constitution was amended several times, a constitutional convention was assembled to write a new basic law. No consensus emerged from differences of opinion, so Kamehameha V abrogated the constitution in 1864. Relying on Caucasian advisers, he proclaimed a new constitution later that year in which voting was restricted on the basis of literacy as well as property ownership or wealth. The new constitution created a unicameral Legislative Assembly, consisting of appointive nobles and elected representatives. As a result, the king increased his power but still wielded a veto (Kuykendall 1938:133).

However, in 1887, King Kalākaua was forced to sign the Bayonet Constitution, which disfranchised those born in Asia (but not Europe, Hawai'i, or the United States), even if they were citizens of Hawai'i. The constitution also increased property qualifications. In the restored bicameral legislature, Caucasians were ensured control: the House of Nobles was to be elected from those with substantial resources in either property or income (no longer appointed by the king), and to serve without pay. There also was a property or income requirement to run for the House of Representatives. The new constitution gave the legislature the power to override a veto by the king if two-thirds of the body so voted. The king thenceforth needed legislative authorization before deploying troops. Although the "bill of rights" clauses remained as before, a new crime was identified – disrespectful behavior or comments about the legislature.

The constitutional legacy consisted of a strong bill of rights, checks and balances between the branches of government, and even the election of monarchs from the royal line. Among various government reforms, Hawai'i established the world's first Board of Health and abolished the death penalty.

White racist influence, responsible for voting qualifications other than age, cannot be considered a part of the legacy. The Bayonet Constitution was contrary to the wishes of the local population, and would not be reinstituted if the kingdom were to be restored at some time in the future.

Remarkable marriage practices

One successful way to bind together a society of persons with different backgrounds is for them to intermarry, have children, and enjoy the diversity. Marrying outside one's group is a way to learn from a different culture in the most intimate manner possible.

It is possible that shipwrecked Japanese and visiting Spanish who arrived in the Islands before 1778 married and produced mixed-race children with the Native Hawaiians, but there is no evidence yet from DNA testing. In any case, Captain Cook's crew was delighted when local women greeted them, though their inevitable offspring did not immediately come forward to announce their dual ancestries.

In 1790, John Young went ashore from one of the early merchant ships. Because of his consummate navigational skills, Kamehameha befriended him but would not let him reboard. Treated well, Young became an adviser to the king, was appointed governor of the island of Hawai'i, and married a local woman. Although Young may not have entered the first biracial marriage in the Islands, the pairing set the tone.

When the missionaries arrived in the 1820s, chiefs suggested that their unattached daughters would make excellent wives for the king's sons, Liholiho and Lot (later Kamehameha IV and V). But their invitations were summarily rejected. When one bachelor missionary married a local girl, he was even suspended from the mission (Daws 1968:114). However, merchants from Europe and the United States had no such qualms. When Chinese were imported to work in the sugarcane fields, they brought no women. The king hoped that some Native Hawaiians would marry Chinese. And intermarry they did – with the blessing of the king (Adams 1933:151). Statistics reveal that about 10 percent of the population was racially mixed, known as "hapa," by the end of the nineteenth century (Schmitt 1965).

Polygamy, commonly practiced by the Native Hawaiian nobles, was abolished by Kamehameha III during the mid-nineteenth century. The kings had male concubines, but of course no "gay marriage." Such behavior was disapproved by the missionaries.

A unique Native Hawaiian practice involves the swapping of children between families. If, for example, a family has seven children and lives next door to a husband and wife unable to have children despite their best efforts, then the former family may give up the care of a son or daughter, in some cases in anticipation of birth, to the latter. The child thus transferred is known as a hānai child (cf. Lancaster 2015:69). No documents are signed, so the practice is different from legal adoption. Customary law in the continental United States would insist that hānai children would be considered wards of the state; hānai adoption was banned by an American court decision in 1901, but never enforced. The size of the hānai population is unknown, but it probably does not seriously affect statistical tabulations. The practice demonstrates how much the culture of the Islands puts social harmony and personal serenity above values that characterize more individualistic societies.

Economic and infrastructure progress

One of the first responses to outside influence was the demarcation of the streets of Honolulu in 1837. The city's first police department was established in 1846. The fire department followed in 1850. Thereafter, fire and police fire departments were established in the other counties. Unlike the other forty-nine states, there is no statewide fire or police department.

The Reciprocity Treaty of 1876 brought so much prosperity to the sugar interests that they no longer needed loans in advance of annual harvests. The Kingdom of Hawaiʻi, thus, because the first Third World country to achieve First World status. However, the result was that the sugar interests were economically dominant in the Islands and would remain so until a few years after World War II.

In 1878, Honolulu resident Charles Dickey bought two telephones while on the continental United States so that he could talk between his home and his office. Hawaiian Telephone Company was established five years later to provide service. Soon, cables were established to link the Islands.

The Islands also became a testing ground for electricity. In 1879, Thomas Edison invented the first cost-effective incandescent lamp. Word of the invention spread to Hawai'i, notably to King Kalākaua, who had a "technical and scientific bent" (Hawaiian Electric 2013). In 1881, the king arranged a meeting with Edison, as he was eager to import the new invention to the Islands. After London and New York began to electrify in 1882, Charles Otto Berger brought Edison's lamps to Honolulu for a demonstration at 'Iolani Palace in 1886. One night, after placing the lamps throughout the palace, they were lit all at once. A crowd gathered, and the Royal Hawaiian Band quickly assembled to celebrate the event. Soon after the world's first steam turbine had been developed in 1884, a steam engine was installed to generate electricity on a regular basis for the lamps at the palace. It should be noted that 'Iolani Palace was lighted by electricity before the White House in Washington, DC.

In 1888, plans for the illumination of downtown Honolulu, then a city of some 23,000 residents, came to fruition. A power plant was built in Nu'uanu Valley, with turbines driven by a hydropower. By 1890, electric power had been extended to nearly 800 businesses and homes. Power plants with generators, some operated by hydropower, were soon built around the Islands, including the plantations, and were consolidated into grids on each island by corporations, such as Hawaiian Electric on O'ahu.

Environmental progress

A law passed in 1839 that prohibited the harvesting of sandalwood trees was superseded in 1846 by a nationalization of all forests. In 1876, the legislature adopted the Act for the Protection and Preservation of Woods and Forests, one component of which was to protect the watershed. To the present, Native Hawaiians consider all land sacred, and they continue to protest efforts to convert pristine land into commercial developments.

Educational progress

Soon after the Hawaiian language became a written language, thanks to efforts of Protestant missionaries from the 1820s, public schools were established, and Hawai'i in 1841 was the first country to offer primary education for all whose parents could pay modest tuition. English was accepted, not imposed, as the medium of instruction soon afterward. As a result, two-thirds of Native Hawaiians were literate by the 1890s (Daws 1968:284).

In addition, the peoples of the Islands value their past. In 1872, the Hawai'i National Museum was founded by Kamehameha V. In 1889, the Bishop

Museum was founded to house heirlooms of the Kamehameha dynasty, received the content of the former museum, and eventually expanded to include other artifacts.

Conclusion

From the earliest Western contact until statehood, the Islands were eager for progress, while still adhering to the norms of the Aloha Spirit. Economist Thomas Hitch (1992:27–8) praises the changes in the following terms:

> Magna cartas to end despotisms, constitutions to end absolutisms, and land reforms to end feudalisms are developments that normally require the shedding of a great deal of blood. Hawai'i's achievement of them bloodlessly on the initiative of the ruling elite is possibility unique in world history. The earlier voluntary abolition of the kapu system, which displaced a long-established religion without a religious war, was another example of the remarkable ability of the early Hawaiian leadership to take bold action when they decided that it was desirable. These acts were even more remarkable because each reduced considerably the power of the ruling group that initiated it.

As a result of forward-thinking Kamehameha the Great, modern military technology was utilized to halt the never-ending civil war and bring unity to the Islands. In 1819, women's rights were asserted by a woman with no direct claim to the throne. Religious freedom dawned in 1839 because the monarchs did not want any more religious disputation. A bill of rights was proclaimed in 1839 primarily to stop the nobility from mistreating commoners. Hawai'i's first constitution was proclaimed in 1840, and the second constitution a dozen years later. The new capital, Honolulu, was chosen for commercial reasons in 1845. Forest conservation efforts were underway by 1846, and a forest reserve was established in 1876. Commercial developments in agriculture (sugarcane and pineapple) brought wealth to the Islands. In the 1880s, Honolulu was one of the first cities in the world lighted by electric power. In other words, the Islands quickly became a part of the modern world without any trace of racism. But the specter of White racism emerged, and the world has forgotten about the halcyon days of the Kingdom of Hawai'i. But lessons can still be learned and hope for the world can be derived therein, as provided in the final chapter.

14 A model for the world

Hawai'i was governed wisely but overpowered because of international forces beyond its control. Nowadays, the memory of the kingdom has been relegated to history books, where few authors are willing to extract lessons about the type of governance and associated cultural norms that put people first. That task is undertaken now.

Engineering racial harmony

When Native Hawaiians greeted the British in the first of many visits from 1778, they were engineering racial harmony by practicing the principles of the Aloha Spirit, albeit not self-consciously. Subsequently, the kings and queens did so deliberately by welcoming White missionaries and traders in several ways: They co-opted some into the government. They adopted Christianity from the missionaries. They wrote democratic constitutions and humane laws that encoded the spirit of Aloha into a legal framework brought by missionary descendants. They encouraged intermarriage. They adopted technological and other innovations. And they lived, shopped, and socialized alongside the newcomers without discrimination.

The main lesson of the kingdom is cultural: transform everyday life to be consistent with Aloha, and racial harmony will result. The consequences of racial harmony were governmental actions and social practices that proved that belief in Aloha can bring about the good life.

The assertion of royal power after the consolidation of the monarchy put the nobility on notice that they could not mistreat commoners and foreigners. Feudalism was abolished in favor of capitalism and private ownership of property.

But economic change inevitably threatened racial harmony. By the end of the nineteenth century, the profit-seeking imperative of White businesses increasingly sought political power to enhance their interests. Whites sought to make non-Whites subordinate. Thus, they engaged in reverse racial engineering – dismantling racial equality to create racist institutions, beginning with the Provisional Government (1893), the Republic of Hawai'i (1894–1898), a two-year period as a colony of the United States (1898–1900), and the Territory of Hawai'i (1900–1959). Racist institutions continued after statehood until questioned in the 1970s, but that is a story for another volume.

Today, one political party in the United States still articulates Social Darwinistic principles (Haas 2010:ch5) and blocks efforts of the other political party to achieve greater racial equality. Within Europe, Christian and secular principles have been insufficient to remedy discrimination against immigrants (Wikan 2002). The Middle East and parts of Africa are aflame with ethnoreligious conflict. Some Asian countries have discontented minority populations (Haas 2013:ch6). Only Latin America and countries in the South Pacific seem peaceful.

The urgency of achieving racial harmony is obvious today. But how can the lessons of the Kingdom of Hawai'i be learned elsewhere? Where racial harmony does not exist, attitudes, norms, policies, and practices can change. Because new norms can be diffused, reverse cultural engineering (unlearning of divisive norms and replacement by harmonious norms) can take place. But how and in what form?

Attitudinal and cultural change to adopt Aloha

Culture is usually defined as an interdependent set of beliefs, customs, habits, laws, and moral principles that are ingrained in a person's psyche from childhood (cf. Tyler 1871). Resolving race relations problems requires an attitude of racial equality, not a belief that one race is superior to another. Unfortunately, some political systems are afflicted by a Darwinistic view that some races have better genes or are more moral than others, while others have racial elites that prefer to preserve dominance while admitting other races to do menial labor and do not allow the latter to rise in social mobility. Indeed, plantation owners in Hawai'i subscribed to Social Darwinism (Porteus 1962; cf. Hofstadter 1955), whereas Native Hawaiians were equalitarians, relying on the Aloha Spirit.

Accordingly, the world must consider that adoption of the culture of Aloha would be one way to bring about greater racial harmony. Learning about how the Kingdom of Hawai'i responded to challenges with humane rather than hierarchical solutions, the focus of the present volume, may serve to popularize the idea that racial harmony is achievable only when elitism and Social Darwinism are abandoned in favor of a belief that the culture of Aloha is a model that can be spread to the world. Attitudes, after all, are prior to behavior. But attitude change is not easily accomplished.

Attitude change goes through four intellectual phase: (1) adoption of an attitude; (2) the attitude is challenged or questioned; (3) unlearning of the attitude; (4) a new attitude is learned and accepted.

For the Aloha Spirit to spread, there must first be a recognition of failure and abandonment of reasons for the failure. In the United States, for example, there must first be an admission that disrespect in matters of race relations is the problem. A new etiquette of mutual respect must be adopted and advanced by opinion leaders.

According to social psychologist Herbert Kelman (1958), the process of attitude change is accelerated by three possible factors – compliance, identification, and internalization. *Compliance* involves attitude change when the consequences of noncompliance are very adverse, as in totalitarian societies. Attitudes may also change when one person emotionally *identifies* with an admired person or group, as when new residents of the Islands marry longtime residents because they marvel at their more humane outlook on life and seek to emulate them. *Internalization* refers to attitude change by those who find the content of a belief to be intrinsically rewarding, as when logic-minded persons discard a false or illogical idea for one that is supported by evidence or logic so that they can confidently defend their attitude whenever challenged.

The incredible change in public attitudes toward gay marriage provides a relevant illustration. Kept in the closet for more than a century, gays and lesbians suffered discrimination based in part on stereotypes. As public figures outed their gender preferences, while media increasingly portrayed fictional gays and lesbians in a favorable light, attitudes shifted largely through emotional identification, especially among those who personally knew gays or lesbians (Silver 2015). Legal changes, however, required internalization by judges and legislators. Currently, wherever gays and lesbians are allowed to marry, homophobes who accept filing fees for marriage certificates are in a mode of compliance. Florists who refuse to cater to same sex weddings may have to await orders of legal compliance with civil rights statutes as yet unlitigated, but some florists will eagerly sell their wares to make money without changing their attitudes (internalization), while others will accept gay marriage out of admiration (identification) for loving couples or out of internalization because resistance involves economic or some other irrationality.

Attitude change only involves incremental change within individuals. Cultural change is much more complicated than attitude change, involving groups. Cultural change occurs in all societies, sometimes imperceptibly, as people accept innovation and invention (Sen 1999). But few cultures undergo radical change because sociocultural stability is usually more highly valued than endless or rapid acceptance of innovations.

The same three factors in attitude change appear to apply to cultural change. But the impetus for radical or transformative cultural change must be a tectonic shock – imposed compliance through a shift in power; identification, as when an attractive new idea spreads by missionaries, secular or otherwise; or by an intellectual paradigm shift, such as the acceptance of representative democratic rule and rejection of the concept of benign or malign authoritarian feudalism.

Cultural change is more likely to occur endogenously than exogenously. When a new culture is exported, the receiving society may be either colonized (forcing compliance), stimulated by what they see elsewhere (identification), or shocked into abandoning old cultural norms and adopting new norms because otherwise insoluble internal conflicts require adoption of better practices found elsewhere (internalization) to keep the society together. The awareness of other cultural norms and practices is far more likely today because of the advance of globalization. Thus, effective cultural change for race relations must involve emotional identification and/or rational internalization. Since emotional identification means admiration of the successes achieved in Hawai'i despite continuing challenges, those who would favor transformation to the ethos of the Aloha Spirit must gain firsthand exposure in the Islands. But few world leaders and opinion shapers, let alone the general public, will ever move to Hawai'i to experience the awe of pleasant race relations. Norm change requires norm entrepreneurs, and the Islands have no such public advocates.

Accordingly, more practical ways can be employed to effect cultural change involving adoption of the Aloha Spirit in race relations – racial intermarriage (the emotional identification method) or a debate over which racial models are appropriate for achieving racial harmony (the rational internalization method). They are discussed next.

Interracial marriage

One successful way to bind together a society of persons with different backgrounds is for them to intermarry, have children, and enjoy the diversity. That is exactly what happened in Hawai'i, consistent with Kelman's concept of change through emotional identification, though not at first evenly across the races that arrived in the Islands.

The experience of racial intermarriage and family customs before annexation suggests that the challenge of disparate ethnic groups resulting from immigration can be overcome when the indigenous population sees the value, moral and practical, of welcoming newcomers into their homes and family lives. Native Hawaiians, thus, played an extraordinary role in promoting a harmonious society. Through a process of acculturation, children of parents working on the plantations accepted the glorious new culture and then taught their parents. While the process continues in the Islands, the rest of the world needs to learn how to develop harmonious race relations.

For example, the division between Germans and Irish immigrants to the United States during the nineteenth century gradually ended as they inter-married, and the idea of the "melting pot" was based on the expectation that Whites of one background would out-marry other Whites. James Coleman (1966) once predicted that race relations problems would end in the United States if everyone were to marry an African American. Many are indeed of mixed racial background, having been sired by Caucasians or married Native Americans. Unfortunately, the mixed racial background of African Americans has not been properly recognized. The "one drop of blood" rule has relegated almost anyone Black to be classified as African American and to live in communities with other Blacks.

However, that may change: The U.S. census, modified in 1990 to accord with the practice developed during the Kingdom of Hawai'i, allows residents to check off more than one racial background. As a result, there has been an increase in reporting by those who consider themselves "mixed." With the development of DNA testing, as highlighted by a project of Harvard professor Henry Louis Gates, Jr., many who consider themselves White may unknowingly be part Black, and vice versa. When Whites now hiding or unaware of their African heritage take pride in that background, Coleman's vision will advance, but only when a multicultural ethos provides a different perspective on race.

Nowadays, the increasing population in the United States of Mexicans, who of course are mestizos, is creating a rapid increase in racial mixtures (AP 2015). They marry without regard to race, including Blacks (blatinos). The concept of *simpático*, quite similar to that of Aloha (Ramírez-Esparza, Goslin, and Pennebaker 2008), has provided evidence that they contribute to cross-racial understanding (Vives 2015). In the same Gallup Poll that ranks Hawai'i as the happiest state, the top ten happiest countries in the world are in Latin America (Birch 2015). And Mexicans are desegregating American cities (Frey 2014).

Unquestionably, Mexicans will make a major impact upon American culture in the future – through their children interacting with non-Mexicans. Rather than marginalizing British traditions and rejecting American culture, intermarriage by Mexicans gives assurance that both cultures will be honored. As for the suspicion that Mexicans will continue to take low-paying jobs away from nonimmigrant Americans, two Asian American sociologists have concluded, comparing rates of intergenerational progress, that Mexican Americans are the most successful immigrant group today, learning English faster than any other ethnic group in history (Lee and Zhou 2014,

2015; Jacoby 2016). The rise of Mexicans to middle class status has been shorter than almost any other immigrant group in the history of the United States.

But not all Mexicans are immigrants. States of the southwestern states were inhabited by persons from Spain and later México before the United States took over, just as the Hawaiian Islands were recognized as an independent country before 1898. Their smiling faces blend smoothly with others in California. Mexicans share democratic principles with the peoples of the Islands due to common experiences of forcible colonization by the United States.

In other words, intermarriage may be the best route to racial harmony without cognitive efforts to argue the virtues of the multicultural ethos of Hawai'i. The principle is the same, however: persons proud of many ethnic and racial roots will learn how to cooperate at home and in a local community before entering a political arena in which mutual respect will lead to a more harmonious future. But how long must we wait for such a development? Within the United States, Western states are far ahead of Eastern and Southern states in that regard today, and most of the rest of the world lags behind – with the notable exception of Latin America. If intermarriage can establish a precondition to racial harmony, the content of that postcondition must also resemble specific reforms.

Looking back, the Hawaiian monarchs provided a model for the world in race relations by freely and widely out-marrying. Those both part-White and part-Hawaiian supported the kingdom against the pure Whites who sought annexation. Today, half those born in the Islands are from parents with differing racial backgrounds (Honolulu Advertiser 2010), and some have more than four different backgrounds, all of which are equally respected. When such diversity is widely accepted, either through contemporary out-marriages or DNA discoveries of prior mixed racial backgrounds, then racial discord will necessarily be reduced.

But attitudes toward race mixing must change first. There must be a prior sense of Aloha about racial mixtures for such intermarriage to be celebrated. The intellectual debate about the proper model of race relations can go in a new direction.

Debate over racial models

The debate about the preferred method of achieving racial harmony has been going on for more than a century, involving competing models. What is problematic is how to characterize the nature of life in the multiethnic Kingdom of Hawai'i and how to explain relative success in attaining ethnic harmony in analytic terms. Most of the debate, which took place after the fall of the monarchy, has been unaware of the important contribution of people of the Islands.

Social Darwinism emerged in the middle of the nineteenth century among Whites in Hawai'i and elsewhere to justify imperial domination of non-White peoples. After developing his view that nature is always in flux from generation to generation because of several biological principles, Charles Darwin (1871) applied his ideas to humans. Those with their own political agendas, even before Darwin, had used the concept of "survival of the fittest" to buttress a political philosophy. Rather than having endless political conflict over which groups have which rights that government must protect, Herbert Spencer (1855) and others felt that conflicts could be overcome by allowing the most "fit" to rule over the less "fit." But there are two types of Social Darwinists (Haas 2012:ch5): The *libertarians*, believing in the "invisible hand" of Adam Smith (1776), would scale down government so that the unfit would die out naturally. The *triumphalists* would use government to favor the rich and disfavor the poor. To merge the two traditions, Social Darwinists favor a majoritarian form of political rule in which the rich propagandize the masses – engineer a culture – to follow their lead (cf. Hofstadter 1944) – in other words, to manufacture consent (Herman and Chomsky 1988). Social Darwinism took hold among elitist Whites in Hawai'i to justify the fall of the monarchy in 1893.

Assimilationism, a second model of race relations, arose in the United States as a response to a flood of immigrants from Eastern Europe and Italy in the 1890s, with many new customs and languages crowding the gateway cities (Ross 1914). Because of perceived social chaos, the assimilationists demanded that newcomers conform to (emulate) norms of Anglo-American culture; otherwise, they would not get jobs and housing and might even be arrested. As early as 1894, President Theodore Roosevelt (quoted in Mikkelson 2015) promoted the idea of assimilation. Clearly racist, assimilationism remains the only model discussed on television discussion programs today, as if there were no other solution than to demand that newcomers drop their culture to become more British. Debate to establish the legitimacy of assimilationism was minimal, and emotional considerations were downplayed. Assimilationists usually assume that "minorities" are "backward," so the concept was inappropriate to Hawai'i, which already had a progressive state before its overthrow.

Naturalist Michel Guillaume Jean de Crèvecœur (1782), historian Frederick Jackson Turner (1893), and novelist Henry James (1907) advanced *amalgamationism* as an alternative. The idea was popularized and coined by Israel Zangwill in a stage play titled *The Melting Pot* (1909). The idea was that a new "amalgamated" American culture should be developed to replace old ways brought from Europe. In other words, the resolution of ethnic conflicts involved intermarriage among European Americans and a melding of cultures brought from Europe, even British culture, in order to develop a common American culture. But of course they did not advocate racial intermarriage, just intermarriage between European Americans, though White masters had produced mixed-race children by raping Black women on the plantations. Amalgamated America was a utopian idea. To effect reverse cultural engineering from disparate European cultures into an idealized concept of American culture, proponents relied on arguments, not emotions. Amalgamationists hoped for a "color blind" society, something optically impossible.

Not all immigrants, however, were eager to jump into the proverbial melting pot. In a polemic written during the first year of World War I, Edward Ross (1914) published a scathing critique of Italians and Slavs as genetically inferior, Jews as greedy, and their presence in the United States as a rootless proletariat threatening skilled native-born workers and relying on political corruption for their advancement. He decried the fact that these groups had not assimilated to Anglo-American culture.

Reviewing Ross's book, philosopher Horace Kallen (1915,1924) advocated *cultural pluralism*. He believed that an acceptance of diverse cultures coexisting in the United States strengthened rather than jeopardized American solidarity. If one culture insisted on dominating all others, he argued, the result would be continuing disunity and strife. He asserted that assimilationists and amalgamationists not only misrepresented the contributions of immigrant groups, but also ignored fundamental American constitutional principles of equality and justice.

Kallen interpreted Ross, the assimilationists, and the amalgamationists as members of an elite Anglo-Saxon class that was losing its dominance and fighting to protect its prerogatives. The uniqueness of America, Kallen felt, was that many streams of immigrants had been enriching the country for more than a century into a mosaic of cultures. Ethnic groups, according to Kallen, retained what is valuable from their own cultural heritage, while accepting a common political culture in the form of democratic principles – representative government under a rule of law that protects individual liberties.

Cultural pluralism was later attacked for justifying *cultural separatism* – that is, for supporting a transformation to a "nation of nations" similar to Switzerland or a segregated America of ethnically pure residential enclaves. Indeed, perverse cultural separatism is often termed *ultranationalism*. The Jim Crow segregation of Blacks from Whites was an example of cultural separation.

Then came the idea of *integration*. The hypothesis was that racial animosity was a result of negative stereotyping, which in turn was due to limited positive contact in social settings: bring the races in contact together somehow, and stereotyping would stop, whereupon racial friendships would develop. The concept of racial integration in Hawai'i was developed by University of Chicago sociologists. Robert Park (1928, 1938), who went to Hawai'i, based his thinking on what he experienced in the Islands. The result was a campaign for integration that eventually resulted in *Brown v Board of Education*, a Supreme Court decision outlawing segregated schools throughout the United States.

Assimilationists lost again with passage of the Immigration Act of 1965, which invited more Asians and Mexicans into the United States. In 1972, the Supreme Court ordered schools in *Lau v Nichols* (414US563) to assist language minority children, primarily immigrants, through bilingual or English-as-a-second language programs. And the Voting Rights Act of 1975 required ballots printed in the home languages of minorities with substantial numbers in voting districts.

Then *multiculturalism* was trumpeted as the answer to increased diversity, similar to Kallen's idea that distinct cultures could live peacefully side by side (Taylor 1989). But unlike Kallen's separatist argument, multiculturalists analyzed the problem of race relations on the basis of evidence that minorities and newcomers were underappreciated and concluded that they could be better understood through top-down educational innovations. However, histories of ethnic groups and English-as-a-second language innovations were badly designed or bureaucratically implemented (Malik 2015), and sudden changes under the name of multiculturalism rankled the mainstream, which resented being labeled as Americentric, Eurocentric, parochial, prejudiced, or otherwise vilified. For the critics, "multiculturalism" went too far by disrespecting the European heritage of the country (Schlesinger 1991), a criticism now echoed in Europe (Malik 2015). Switzerland was not a model for the multiculturalists; they crafted a utopian idea that was easily criticized. For Amaryta Sen (2006), what had developed was instead *plural monoculturalism*, not unlike Kallen's cultural separatism. They failed to point to any paradigm case except perhaps Canada, where the concept justified acceptance of a bilingual society (Canada 1965).

A final concept, which has not gained mainstream acceptance, is *interculturalism* (Bennett 1998). For interculturalists, ethnic discrimination and racism exist because not all groups receive condign respect. Instead, the population in general should be encouraged to be delighted to learn cultural norms of others, since greater mutual respect will mean that animosities will gradually evaporate. But interculturalism, too, is utopian: most Americans are not interested in learning from persons of other cultures and thus misperceive and discriminate based on their misperceptions or prejudices. Interculturalists appeal to the view that ethic and racial pride should come from the bottom up, unlike top-down multiculturalism.

But the Kingdom of Hawai'i never had to undergo such a debate between alternative models of race relations. Instead, interculturalism was accepted as the basis for welcoming an integrated society. The view was that members of different cultures had been learning from one another rather than having one prevail or allowing diverse cultures to become separatist. Interculturalists, in other words, have been striving to find commonalities and consider differences worthy of respect (Bennett 1998). Thus, groups from Asia retained their cultural norms, often as a rich resource to counter unjust discrimination on the plantations, while accepting American economic and political principles. Interculturalism is particularly meaningful for those who are biracial and multiracial. What was very special in Hawai'i was how members of each culture learned from other cultures, while accepting a unique ethos – the Aloha Spirit – which established common norms of behavior. Even in the present, those with the highest levels of mental health subscribe to the Aloha Spirit and have strong pride in their cultural background (Mossakowski and Wongkaren 2016).

Meanwhile, those who adopted "multiculturalism" without interculturalism have suffered the consequences – stereotypic treatment of minorities, who in turn have failed to advance socioeconomically and blame the majority for their failure to flourish. In Europe, one result has been the emergence of domestic terroristic attacks (Malik 2015).

Clearly, Hawai'i is not a melting pot because the various cultures have retained their different identities. Some have advocated the cultural pluralist analogy of a "stew pot." John McDermott and Naupaka Andrade (2011:321) suggest a "lauhala" model – that is, the way in which several leaves of different colors from the hala tree are combined in making a colorful basket. Helen Chapin (2011:ch5) prefers "mixed plate," referring to a meal with portions on the same platter from several cuisines (American, Chinese, Japanese, and so forth).

Rather than being overwhelmed by diversity, as is often the case on the continental United States and elsewhere, people in Hawai'i celebrate diversity and feel pride that they comprise a kind of United Nations, both because different groups are mutually respectful and because intermarriage has produced a mixture of ancestral backgrounds that are carried by about half of the population. Interculturalism has succeeded because the cultural dialog goes on within families where the ethnic backgrounds of mothers differ from fathers. And both may already be mixed before their first child is born.

Thus, the experience of the Kingdom of Hawai'i is that the Aloha Spirit prevailed, so racial harmony prevailed until White racists relied on Social Darwinism to overthrow the monarchy in order to bring about American colonial domination. To defeat Social Darwinism, non-Whites in the Islands had to campaign for statehood, where they would have a voting majority to reverse White racism. For peoples elsewhere, the debate over types of racial models has scarcely begun.

What the debate over models of race relations stimulates is a question of how to implement the principles into action. There is a need to specify principles about government that can be accepted by the people in the form of basic agreements or compacts.

Societal compacts

Democratic theory, especially in the United States, is rooted in the mythical social contract – a primordial agreement in which the people granted power to government under certain conditions. The first Western philosopher to develop the concept of the social contract was Thomas Hobbes (1651), who believed that people granted unlimited power to government in order to provide social stability. Hobbes opposed democracy, as did Plato (c.360 BCE) and Confucius (cf. Basham 1961:82), fearing that otherwise social chaos would prevail. A similar autocratic social contract has been practiced by proponents of totalitarian rule – Hitler, Mao, and Stalin.

Democratic social contract theory was instead developed by several thinkers. To oversimplify, Jean-Jacques Rousseau (1762) believed that true democracy involves collective decisions in town meetings, which will grant very limited power to government. The social contract theory of John Locke (1688) was premised on the idea that the people can elect legislative representatives to carry out their wishes, provided that government does not tread on inalienable rights of the people. Founders of the United States federal government, such as James Madison (c.1776), believed that the social contract can be stated in the form of a constitution, which grants specific powers to branches of government and retains powers for the people within a bill of rights. However, anarchist Lysander Spooner (c.1876) has famously ridiculed the social contract concept of the United States because although the Constitution was put to a vote in the thirteen onetime British colonies to supersede the Articles of Confederation, African slaves were not allowed to vote and were therefore excluded from, but subject to, the "contract."

Even though democratic theory has developed beyond the social contract approach (cf. Dahl 1971; Rawls 1971; Habermas 1992), one way to understand Hawai'i is as an extension of social contract theory. The Kingdom of Hawai'i developed two social compacts, as described below.

Sociopolitical compact

Adoption of Hawai'i's racial harmony will occur when other places in the world adopt a new sociopolitical compact. What occurred during the monarchy was the enrichment and fulfillment of democratic principles based on the Aloha Spirit:

- A cardinal rule of Island politics is to listen to the views of persons with various deeply held cultural perspectives in an agreeable manner. The constitution of 1840 was the world's third to provide universal adult suffrage and the first to allow women's suffrage.
- Political decisions are made to unite rather than divide, awaiting a consensus in the community on difficult issues; zerosum political victories are abhorrent. The provision for the people to vote for the monarch is case of contested claims to the throne was aimed at healing divisions within the ruling class and the voting public.
- Political leaders give priority to advancing and maintaining racial harmony. Early efforts to include Chinese and Japanese within the voting public served to avoid bitterness within ethnic communities.
- Incremental decisions are preferred over drastic and comprehensive decisions. Government leaders engage in wide consultation so that the lives of ordinarily people will not be suddenly uprooted; their sense of continuity and stability should not be placed in jeopardy. As the first country to offer universal primary education, the government did not impose a compulsory requirement.
- Decisions must advance the quality of human life, show compassion and kindness. Hawai'i was the first country to establish a ministry of health in order to coordinate efforts to combat the various epidemic diseases and the first to abolish the death penalty.

The principles identified above flow from the five principles of the Aloha Spirit, an ethos that is more than just principles of personal etiquette, but instead deeply affects politics. The aim is to make government more sensitive to all racial and religious groups. Many more examples could be used to illustrate each principle.

Environmental compact

Extraordinary measures to preserve the environment in the Islands flow from the view of Native Hawaiians that land and nature have spiritual significance. Adoption of various incremental measures to protect the environment rejected the paradigm that humans are free to exploit nature to their selfish advantage:

- Nature is perceived as an agreeable friend to be cherished rather than an obstacle to be overcome. The development of the ahupua'a allowed farmers to cultivate self-sufficient plots of land from the mountains to the sea, provided that they were productive conservators of the ecosystem.

- Nature came before humans and makes human life possible, so there is a sense of awe about the environment, which cannot be brutalized. Rather than radical methods to eradicate pests, the Kingdom of Hawai'i pioneered in developing what later became the science of tropical agriculture by declaring a moratorium on cutting down trees in the wilderness.
- The beauty of nature is something to humble humans, who cannot compete with such magnificence. The kingdom nationalized forests to end commercial despoliation.
- The environment is considered sacred, something to be monitored with patience and vigilance. Before private property was allowed in the mid-nineteenth century, the kings and chiefs issued kapus to prevent mistreatment of nature.
- Nature is considered a source of harmonious life. Humans must maintain unity with nature, not opposition. The kingdom recognized the right of the people to water in 1860 and set up a board to ensure that water would not be selfishly exploited.

In *This Changes Everything* (2014), Naomi Klein makes a grandiose argument that conscientious attention to saving the planet will ultimately transform economic and political systems. In order to forestall an environmental Armageddon, she points out, several reforms are necessary: agricultural lands need to be redistributed to small farmers. Alternative energy sources, which will be vital for the continuation of modern life, will also spark a boom in job creation. Indigenous peoples must have their traditional land rights respected. The rape of nature can no longer be allowed. Sources of fresh water must be rescued from pollution. And the political stranglehold held by corporate power must end. One consequence, she predicts, is to decrease inequality – both within and between nations. Klein's socioenvironmental argument is almost identical with the moral argument of Pope Francis (2015), who is critical of the greed responsible for the despoliation of ecosystems (cf. McKibben 2015). Klein's recommendations could be interpreted as a return to the days of the Kingdom of Hawai'i.

Alas, there was no economic compact during the monarchy on a par with the previous two. The establishment of plantation agriculture on private property operated by Caucasians exploiting non-White workers started slowly but dominated the economy at the end of the nineteenth century. Rights of workers would not be fully recognized until after the Great Depression of the 1930s.

Restoration of independence

Beyond racial intermarriage, adopting of the integration and intercultural models, and the two societal compacts, yet another option for disseminating Aloha would be for the Islands to make a bold international statement by becoming an independent country again. Then the rest of the world, including the other forty-nine states of the United States, could pay more attention to what the Kingdom of Hawai'i achieved. The world would definitely benefit from the voice of Hawai'i in the General Assembly of the United Nations.

Independence seems warranted under international law, though the idea has not yet gained traction in an international tribunal. The impropriety of the overthrow of the monarchy in 1893 has been acknowledged by the Apology Resolution adopted by Congress and signed by President Bill Clinton in 1993. Annexation of the Hawaiian Islands in 1898 occurred without a plebiscite or a treaty. President Grover Cleveland and members of Congress then believed that annexation was contrary to international law. The option of independence has never been on the ballot. Such a plebiscite might today gain a majority, especially from those who want to return to the days of the monarchy.

Native Hawaiians took special note as Slovakia seceded from Czechoslovakia in 1993. The vote for Scottish independence in 2014 suggested that even a conservative British government would listen to the call for self-determination by allowing a plebiscite in the twenty-first century. As an independent country, Hawai'i's voice would be more likely to be heard than the present situation, in which the Islands are submerged within a country that has failed to learn the lessons about racial harmony that are embedded within the history of the Kingdom of Hawai'i. Just as the kings and queens played leadership roles in spreading Aloha throughout the kingdom, a UN Secretary General from the Islands could be a leader in showing the world how Aloha works to bring racial and other forms of harmony.

Conclusion

For many Hawai'i residents and members of the rest of the world, the picture painted herein may seem far too idealized. Politics is a rough-and-tumble sport, economies are fragile, and the ecosystem is precarious. But it never occurred to Native Hawaiians to be anything but friendly and helpful to everyone and everything.

Indeed, the Kingdom of Hawai'i was ahead of its time. Current attitudes of individualism and unilateralism are out of touch with the realities of a truly interdependent world today. In diffusing new norms, there must be receptivity by norm takers. Discarding (pruning) the inapplicable traits of the past will occur when the world realizes that a coherent community-oriented culture is needed. For a model, there is one in the middle of the Pacific.

When racial problems emerge nowadays, the usual model invoked is the model of social integration derived from the experience in Hawai'i – that is, bringing persons of different backgrounds into contact with one another. But someone is likely to get wet walking down the street during a torrential rainstorm with only a rain hat because they need an umbrella, a raincoat, and even rain shoes. Relying solely on social integration may get one wet in a racial uprising. The lesson of the Kingdom of Hawai'i is that integration worked because there was prior racial intermarriage, residential racial integration, and cultural norms favoring such behavior, including an intercultural version of the social contract applied to the environment and politics. Within the United States, a Supreme Court decision requiring school integration without the other conditions being present resulted in "White flight" – that is, the rejection of the imperative of cultural learning by a movement of Whites to the suburbs, with many African Americans left marooned in the urban areas.

What was different about the Kingdom of Hawai'i is *how* problems were perceived, *how* challenges were handled, *how* people related to one another, and *how* government acted with cultural sensitivity: acrimony was minimal. Nobody was demonized. Problems were ultimately resolved, sometimes quietly and slowly, rather than being allowed to fester indefinitely. Mutual respect kept everyone smiling. Most of those who move to the Islands over the centuries have learned how Aloha is truly contagious.

For cynics who believe that the Aloha Spirit cannot work outside the Islands where conditions are different, the fact is that racism is primarily an attitude that generates a set of exclusionary conditions. Those in the United States who believe that racism exists because there is a "Black problem" should look in the mirror – at the White problem – and start removing those conditions after rejecting associated racist attitudes and developing a spirit of Aloha toward all.

Even if the world remains deaf to the norms of Aloha, the encouragement of racial intermarriage and racial integration in the larger society by those who carry norms similar to those of Aloha will result in a new cultural climate to challenge those who prefer racial disharmony. Direct norm change can occur through persuasion (internalization), but integrative behaviors can modify attitudes indirectly by socialization – attracting emulation with those who carry the message (identification).

Now, dear reader, it's your turn to spread Aloha for the benefit of the world. The torch of how to achieve racial harmony has been passed to you.

Are you willing to carry that torch? Are you willing to make the necessary adjustment to a new set of cultural principles and convince others to do the same? As Reinhold Niebuhr (2015:705) once said, do you have the "courage to change the things that should be changed"? Do you really want to see racial conflicts resolved? The future depends on your courage and fortitude.

Bibliography

Adams, Romanzo C. (1933). "The Unorthodox Race Doctrine of Hawai'i." In *Race and Culture Contacts*, ed. E. B. Reuter, pp. 143–60. New York: McGraw-Hill.

Akaka, Daniel (2009). "Address to Congress," *Congressional Record*, 155 (154): S8210–11, July 28.

Andrews, Lorrin (1865). *A Dictionary of the Hawaiian Language*. Honolulu: Island Heritage Publishing, 2003.

Appiah, Kwame Anthony (2015). "Race in the Modern World: The Problem of the Color Line," *Foreign Affairs*, 94 (2): 1–10.

Asato, Laureen R. (1981). *Coverture, the Right to Contract, and the Status of Women in Hawai'i: Pre-Contact to 1888*. Master's Thesis, Department of Sociology, University of Hawai'i at Mānoa.

Associated Press (1959). "Eisenhower Says Hawai'i's Showcase of Brotherhood," *Honolulu Star-Bulletin*, December 10: 1.

Associated Press (2015). "New Census May Mean Fewer 'Whites'," *Los Angeles Times*, December 20.

Barrett, Glynn (1988). *The Russian View of Honolulu, 1809–26*. Ottawa, Canada: Carleton University Press.

Basham, A. I. (1961). *The Wonder That Was India: A Survey of the History and Culture of the Indian Sub-Continent Before the Coming of the Muslims*. London: Sidgwick & Jackson.

Beechert, Edward D. (1985). *Working in Hawai'i*. Honolulu: University of Hawai'i Press.

Beechert, Edward D. (1992). "Hawaiian Labor: The Social Relations of Production." In *Politics and Public Policy in Hawai'i*, eds. Zachary A. Smith and Richard C. Pratt, Chapter 14. Albany: State University of New York Press.

Beechert, Edward D. (2011). "The Strength of Organized Labor." In *Barack Obama, the Aloha Zen President: How a Son of the 50th State May Transform America Based on 12 Multicultural Principles*, ed. Michael Haas, Chapter 9. Santa Barbara, CA: Praeger.

Bennett, Judith M., and C. Warren Hollister (2006). *Medieval Europe: A Short History*. New York: McGraw-Hill.

Bennett, Milton J. (1998) *Basic Concepts of Intercultural Communication*. Boston: Intercultural Press.

Bickerton, Derek (1998). "Language and Language Contact." In *Multicultural Hawai'i: The Fabric of a Multiethnic Society*, ed. Michael Haas, Chapter 3. New York: Garland.

Birch, Janice (2015). "The Country with the Happiest People Is . . ., " yahoo.com, March 20. Accessed March 20, 2015.

Blaisdell, Kekuni, Nālani Minton, and Ulla Hasager (2014). "Ka Hoʻokolokolnui Kānaka Maoli, 1993: The Peoples' International Tribunal, Hawai'i." In *A Nation Rising: Hawaiian Movements for Life, Land, and Sovereignty*, eds. Noelani Goodyear-Kaʻōpua, Ikaika Hussey, and Erin Kahunawaikaʻala Wright, Chapter 13. Durham, NC: Duke University Press.

Blount, James (1893). *Papers Relating to the Mission of James Blount*. Washington, DC: Government Printing Office.

Boylan, Dan (1992). "Blood Runs Thick: Ethnicity as a Factor in Hawai'i's Politics." In *Politics and Policy in Hawai'i*, eds. Zachary A. Smith and Richard C. Pratt, Chapter 4. Albany: State University of New York Press.

Brieske, Philip R. (1961). *A Study of the Development of Public Elementary and Secondary Education in the Territory of Hawai'i*. Seattle: Ph.D. dissertation, University of Washington.

Brooks, David (2015). *The Road to Character*. New York: Random House.

Buck, Peter (1953). *Vikings in the Pacific*. Chicago, IL: University of Chicago Press.

Budnick, Rich (2005). *Hawai'i's Forgotten History, 1900–1999: The Good . . . the Bad . . . the Embarrassing*. Honolulu: Aloha Press.

Burrows, Edwin G. (1947). *Hawaiian Americans: An Account of the Mingling of Japanese, Chinese, Polynesian, and American Cultures*. New Haven, CT: Yale University Press.

Cabin, Robert J. (2013). *Restoring Paradise: Rethinking and Rebuilding Nature in Hawai'i*. Honolulu: University of Hawai'i Press.

Canada, Royal Commission on Bilingualism and Biculturalism (1965). *Report*. Ottawa: Royal Commission on Bilingualism and Biculturalism.

Cayetano, Benjamin J. (2009). *Ben: A Memoir, From Street Kid to Governor*. Honolulu: Watermark.

Chapin, Helen Geracimos (2011). "The Media: A Mixed Plate." In *Barack Obama, the Aloha Zen President; How a Son of the 50th State May Revitalize America Based on 12 Multicultural Principles*, ed. Michael Haas, Chapter 5. Santa Barbara, CA: Praeger.

Charlot, Jean (1970). "An 1849 Hawaiian Broadside," *Hawaiian Journal of History*, 4: 96–104.

Chun, Malcolm Nāea (2011). *No Nā Mamo: Traditional and Contemporary Hawaiian Beliefs and Practices*. Honolulu: University of Hawai'i Press.

Clement, Russell (1980). "From Cook to the 1840 Constitution: The Name Change from Sandwich to Hawaiian Islands," *Hawaiian Journal of History*, 14: 50–7.

Coffman, Tom (2003). *The Island Edge of America: A Political History of Hawai'i*. Honolulu: University of Hawai'i Press.

Coleman, James S., et al. (1966). *On Equality of Educational Opportunity*. Washington, DC. Government Printing Office.

Conan, Katherine (1946). *The History of Contract Labor in the Hawaiian Islands*. Princeton, NJ: Princeton University Press.

Connelly, Sean (2014). "Urbanism as Island Living." In *The Value of Hawai'i 2: Ancestral Roots, Oceanic Visions*, eds. Aiko Yamashiro and Noelani Goodyear-Ka'ōpua, pp. 188–99. Honolulu: University of Hawai'i Press.

Cullenney, John L. (2006). *Islands in a Far Sea: The Fate of Nature in Hawai'i.* Honolulu: University of Hawai'i Press.

Curtis, Henry (2010). "Energy." In *The Value of Hawai'i: Knowing the Past, Shaping the Future*, eds. Craig Howes and Jon Osorio, pp. 179–86. Honolulu: University of Hawai'i Press.

Dahl, Robert A. (1971). *Polyarchy, Participation, and Opposition.* New Haven, CT: Yale University Press.

Darwin, Charles (1871). *The Descent of Man, and Selection in Relation to Sex.* London: John Murray.

Daws, Gavan (1968). *Shoal of Time: A History of the Hawaiian Islands.* New York: Macmillan.

de Crèvecœur, Michel Guillaume Jean (1782). *Letters from an American Farmer.* London: Davies.

Deerr, Noel (1949). *The History of Sugar.* London: Chapman and Hall.

Diamond, J. M. (1997). *Guns, Germs and Steel: The Fates of Human Societies.* New York: Norton.

Dougherty, Michael (1992). *To Steal a Kingdom: Probing Hawaiian History.* Waimānalo, HI: Island Style Press.

Dudley, Michael Kioni (1990). *Man, Gods, and Nature.* Honolulu: Na Kane O Ka Malo Press.

Dudley, Michael Kioni, and Keoni Kealoha Agard (1990). *A Call for Hawaiian Sovereignty.* Honolulu: Na Kane or Ka Malo Press.

Dunning, Nicholas P., and Timothy Beach (1994). "Soil Erosion, Slope Management, and Ancient Terracing in the Maya Lowlands," *Latin American Antiquity*, 5 (1): 51–69.

Eagar, Harry (1997). "PASH Access Law Raises Many Questions," *Maui News*, October 10.

Eisinger, Peter K. (1988). *The Politics of Displacement.* New York: Academic Press.

Elbert, Samuel H., and Mary Kawena Pukui (1954). *Hawaiian Grammar.* Honolulu: University Press of Hawai'i.

Engels, Friedrich (1884). *The Origin of the Family, Private Property and the State.* New York: Pathfinder, 1972.

Ferguson, Kathy, and Phyllis Turnbull (2010). "The Military." In *The Value of Hawai'i: Knowing the Past, Shaping the Future*, eds. Craig Howes and Jon Osorio, pp. 47–52. Honolulu: University of Hawai'i Press.

Finney, Ben R. (1973). *Polynesian Peasants and Proletarians.* Cambridge, MA: Schenkman.

Forbes, David W. (1991). "Look the Rock Whence Ye Are Hewn: A Reappraisal of Punahou's Earlier History." In *Punahou: The History and Promise of a School of the Islands*, ed. Nelson Foster, pp. 119–49. Honolulu: Punahou School.

Fornander, Abraham (1880). *An Account of the Polynesian Race.* Volume 2. London: Trübner.

Francis, John M. (2005). *Iberia and the Americas Culture, Politics, and History: A Multicultural Encyclopedia.* Santa Barbara, CA: ABC-CLIO.

Frey, William H. (2014). *Diversity Explosion: How Racial Demographics Are Remaking America*. Washington, DC: Brookings Institution Press.

The Friend (1849). November 15.

Fuchs, Lawrence H. (1961). *Hawai'i Pono: A Social History*. Glencoe, IL: Free Press.

Geschwender, James A. (1982). "The Hawaiian Transformation: Class, Submerged Nation, and National Minorities." In *Ascent and Decline in the World-System*, ed. Edward Friedman, Chapter 8. Beverly Hills, CA: Sage.

Gething, Judith R. (1977). "Christianity and Coverture: Impact on the Legal Status of Women in Hawai'i, 1820–1920," *Hawaiian Journal of History*, 11: 188–220.

Glazer, Nathan (1987). *Affirmative Discrimination: Ethnic Inequality and Public Policy*. New York: Basic Books.

Glick, Clarence E. (1980). *Sojourners and Settlers: Chinese Migrants in Hawai'i*. Honolulu: University Press of Hawai'i.

Gray, Francine du Plessix (1972). *Hawai'i: The Sugar-Coated Fortress*. New York: Vintage.

Green, James R. (2006). *Death in the Haymarket: A Story of Chicago, the First Labor Movement and the Bombing That Divided Gilded Age America*. New York: Pantheon.

Haas, Michael (1992). *Institutional Racism: The Case of Hawai'i*. Westport, CT: Praeger.

Haas, Michael, ed. (1998). *Multicultural Hawai'i: The Fabric of a Multiethnic Society*. New York: Garland.

Haas, Michael (2010). *Looking for the Aloha Spirit: Promoting Ethnic Harmony*. Los Angeles: Publishinghouse for Scholars.

Haas, Michael (2012). *Mr. Calm and Effective: Evaluating the Presidency of Barack Obama*. Los Angeles: Publishinghouse for Scholars.

Haas, Michael (2013). *Asian and Pacific Cooperation: Turning Zones of Conflict into Arenas of Peace*. New York: Palgrave Macmillan.

Haas, Michael (2014a). *International Human Rights: A Comprehensive Introduction*. 2nd edn. New York: Routledge.

Haas, Michael (2014b). *Neobehavioral Political Science: A Profession's Fascinating History, Subfields, Paradigms, Research Agenda, Policy Applications, and Future*. Los Angeles: Publishinghouse for Scholars.

Haas, Michael, and Peter P. Resurrection, eds. (1976). *Politics and Prejudice in Contemporary Hawai'i*. Honolulu: Coventry Press.

Habermas, Jürgen (1992). *Between Facts and Norms: Contributions to a Discourse Theory of Law and Democracy*. Cambridge, MA: MIT Press.

Handy, E. S. Craighill (1965). "Race." In *Ancient Hawaiian Civilization: A Series of Lectures Delivered at the Kamehameha Schools*, Chapter 1. Rev. edn. Rutland, VT: Tuttle, 1970.

Handy, E. S. C., and E. G. Handy (1972). *Native Planters in Old Hawai'i: Their Life, Lore and Environment*. Honolulu: Bishop Museum Press.

Handy, E. S. C., and M. K. Pukui (1972). The *Polynesian Family System in Ka'u Hawai'i*. Tokyo: Tuttle.

Harris, Marvin (1968). *The Rise of Anthropological Theory: A History of Theories of Culture*. New York: Crowell.

Hawai'i, Republic of (1895). *Report of the Labor Commissioner on Strikes and Arbitration*. Honolulu: Labor Commission, Republic of Hawai'i.

Hawai'i, Republic of (1896). *Biennial Report of the Board of Education*. Honolulu: Board of Education, Republic of Hawai'i.

Hawai'i, State of, Department of Business, Economic Development, and Tourism (1993). *Data Book: A Statistical Abstract*. Honolulu: Department of Business, Economic Development, and Tourism.

Hawai'i, State of, Department of Business, Economic Development and Tourism (2006). *Data Book: A Statistical Abstract*. Honolulu: Department of Business, Economic Development, and Tourism.

Hawai'i, State of, Department of Business, Economic Development and Tourism (2013). *Data Book: A Statistical Abstract*. Honolulu: Department of Business, Economic Development, and Tourism.

Hawaiian Electric (2013). *Heco: About Us, Our Story.* Honolulu: Hawaiian Electric, www.hawaiianelectric.com/heco/About-US/Our-Story. Accessed June 14, 2014.

Hawaiian Sugar Planters' Association (1926). *The Story of Sugar in Hawai'i*. Honolulu: HSPA.

Hazama, Dorothy Ochiai, and Jane Okamoto Kameji (1986). *Okage Sama De: The Japanese in Hawai'i, 1885–1985*. Honolulu: Bess Press.

Hendricks, Lyle E., James Mak, and G. Tamaribuchi (1989). *Hawai'i's Economy*. Honolulu: Department of Education, State of Hawai'i.

Herman, Edward S., and Noam Chomsky (1988). *Manufacturing Consent: The Political Economy of the Mass Media*. New York: Pantheon.

Hitch, Thomas Kemper (1992). *Islands in Transition: The Past, Present, and Future of Hawai'i's Economy*. Honolulu: First Hawaiian Bank.

Hobbes, Thomas (1651). *Leviathan: On the Matter, Forme, and Power of a Common-Wealth Ecclesiasticall and Civill*. New Haven, CT: Yale University Press, 2010.

Hofstadter, Richard (1944). *Social Darwinism in American Thought*. Rev. Edn. Boston: Beacon, 1955.

Honolulu Advertiser (2010). "Hawai'i Still Leads U.S. with Highest Rate of Mixed Marriages," *Honolulu Advertiser*, May 27.

Honolulu Independent (1899). "Chinese Strikers on Maui," *Honolulu Independent*, January 10.

Honolulu Japanese Chamber of Commerce (1970). *The Rainbow: A Bridge from East to West, Past to Future*. Honolulu: Honolulu Japanese Chamber of Commerce.

Hoover, Will (2009). "Better Count Needed for Hawaiians," *Honolulu Advertiser*, August 7.

Hope, Bradley E., and Janette Harbottle Hope (2003). "Native Hawaiian Health in Hawai'i: Historical Highlights," *California Journal of Health Promotion*, 1 (Special Issue): 1–9.

Howard, Alan (1974). *Ain't No Big Thing: Coping Strategies in a Hawaiian American Community*. Honolulu: University of Hawai'i Press.

Huntington, Samuel P. (2004). *Who Are We? The Challenges to America's National Identity*. New York: Simon & Schuster.

Jacoby, Tamar (2016). "Advancing Beyond Survival English," *Los Angeles Times*, January 5.

James, Henry (1907). *The American Scene*. London: Chapman & Hall.

Kallen, Horace (1915). "Democracy Versus the Melting Pot," *The Nation*, 100 (February 18, 25): 190–4, 217–22.

Kallen, Horace (1924). *Culture and Democracy in the United States*. New York: Liveright.

Kamakau, Samuel (1964). *The People of Old*. Honolulu: Bishop Museum Press.

Kamakau, Samuel (1976). *The Works of the People of Old*. Honolulu: Bishop Museum Press.

Kane, Herb Kawainui (1997). *Ancient Hawai'i*. Honolulu: Kawaihui Press.

Kame'eleihiwa, Lilikala (1992). *Native Land and Foreign Desires: Pehea Lā E Pono Ai?* Honolulu: Bishop Museum Press.

Kanahele, George He'ue Sanford (1986). *Ku Kanaka Stand Tall: A Search for Hawaiian Values*. Honolulu: University of Hawai'i Press.

Kauanui, J. Kēhaulani (2014). "Resisting the Akaka Bill." In *A Nation Rising: Hawaiian Movements for Life, Land, and Sovereignty*, eds. Noelani Goodyear-Ka'ōpua, Ikaika Hussey, and Erin Kahunawaika'ala Wright, Chapter 15. Durham, NC: Duke University Press.

Kealoha-Scullion, Kehaulani K. (1995). *The Hawaiian Journey: Out of the Case of Identity, Images of the Hawaiian and Other*. Honolulu: Ph.D. dissertation, University of Hawai'i.

Kelleher, Jennifer Sinco (2015). "Some Native Hawaiians Disapprove of 'Aloha' Movie Title," *Honolulu Star-Advertiser*, May 25.

Kelly, Marion (1956). *Changes in Land Tenure in Hawai'i, 1778–1850*. Honolulu: M.A. Thesis, University of Hawai'i.

Kelly, Marion (1972). *Demography of the Hawaiian Islands*. Honolulu: Bishop Museum.

Kelman, Herbert C. (1958). "Compliance, Identification, and Internalization: Three Processes of Attitude Change," *Journal of Conflict Resolution*, 2 (1): 51–60.

Kent, Noel J. (1983). *Hawai'i: Islands under the Influence*. New York: Monthly Review Press.

Klein, Naomi (2014). *This Changes Everything: Capitalism vs. the Climate*. New York: Simon & Schuster.

Kuykendall, Ralph A. (1938). *The Hawaiian Kingdom, 1778–1854*. Volume I. Honolulu: University of Hawai'i Press.

Kuykendall, Ralph A. (1938). The *Hawaiian Kingdom, 1774–1893*. Volume III. Honolulu: University of Hawai'i Press.

La Croix, Sumner (2010). "The Economy." In *The Value of Hawai'i: Knowing the Past, Shaping the Future*, eds. Craig Howes and Jon Osorio, pp. 23–30. Honolulu: University of Hawai'i Press.

Lancaster, John (2015). "Pure Hawaiian," *National Geographic*, 227 (2): 54–77.

Lebo, Susan A. (2010). "A Local Perspective of Hawai'i's Whaling Economy: Whale Traditions and Government Regulations of the Kingdom's Native Seamen and Whale Fishery," *Interdisciplinary Journal of Maritime Studies*, ijms.nmdl. org/article/view/5805/4017.

Lee, Jennifer, and Min Zhou (2014). "The Success Frame and Achievement Paradox: The Cost and Consequences for Asian-Americans," *Race and Social Problems*, 6 (1): 38–55.

Lee, Jennifer, and Min Zhou (2015). *The Asian American Achievement Paradox.* New York: Russell Sage.

Lili'uokalani, Lydia (1898). *Hawai'i's Story by Hawai'i's Queen.* Tokyo: Tuttle, 1964.

Lind, Andrew W. (1938). *An Island Community: Ecological Succession in Hawai'i.* Chicago: University of Chicago Press.

Lind, Andrew W. (1967). *Hawai'i's People.* 3rd edn. Honolulu: University of Hawai'i Press.

Lind, Andrew W. (1969). *Hawai'i: The Last of the Magic Isles.* New York: Oxford University Press.

Lind, Andrew W. (1980). *Hawai'i's People.* 4th edn. Honolulu: University of Hawai'i Press.

Lindo, Cecilia Kapua, and Nancy Alpert Mower, eds. (1980). *Polynesian Seafaring Heritage.* Honolulu: Kamehameha Schools Press.

Lindsay, Almont (1943). *The Pullman Strike: The Story of a Unique Experiment and of a Great Labor Upheaval.* Chicago, IL: University of Chicago Press.

Locke, John (1688). *Second Treatise of Government.* Cambridge, UK: Cambridge University Press, 1967.

MacKenzie, Melody Kapilialoha, ed. (1991). *Native Hawaiian Rights Handbook.* Honolulu: Native Hawaiian Legal Corporation.

Madison, James (c.1776). *The Theory and Practice of Republican Government*, ed. Samuel Kernell. Stanford, CA: Stanford University Press, 2003.

Malik, Kenan (2015). "The Failure of Multiculturalism: Community Versus Society in Europe," *Foreign Affairs*, 94 (2): 21–32.

McDermott, John F., and Naupaka Andrade (2011). "Conclusion." In *People and Cultures of Hawai'i: The Evolution of Culture and Ethnicity*, eds. John F. McDermott and Naupaka Andrade, pp. 316–34. Honolulu: University of Hawai'i Press.

McGregor, Davianna P. (1991). "Providing Redress for *Ka Po'e Hawai'i*: The Hawaiian People." Paper presented at the Spark M. Matsunaga Institute for Peace Conference on Restructuring for Peace: Challenges for the 21st Century, Honolulu, June 3.

McGregor, Pōmaika'i Davianna, and Noa Emmett Aluli (2014). "Wao Kele O Puna and the Pele Defense Fund." In *A Nation Rising: Hawaiian Movements for Life, Land, and Sovereignty*, eds. Noelani Goodyear-Ka'ōpua, Ikaika Hussey, and Erin Kahunawaika'ala Wright, Chapter 8. Durham, NC: Duke University Press.

McKibben, Bill (2015). "The Pope and the Planet," *New York Review of Books*, 62 (13): 40–2.

McNeill, W. H. (1976). *Plagues and Peoples.* New York: Anchor Press/Doubleday.

Meller, Norman (1958). "Missionaries to Hawai'i: Shapers of the Islands' Government," *Western Political Quarterly*, 11 (4): 788–99.

Meredith, Gerald (1965). "Observations on the Acculturation of Sansei Japanese-Americans in Hawai'i," *Psychologia*, 8 (June): 41–9.

Michener, James (1959). *Hawai'i.* New York: Random House.

Mikkelson, David (2015). "Sole Loyalty," *snopes.com/politics/quotes/roosevelt.asp,* September 23, 2015. Accessed June 8, 2016.

Moore, Susanna (2015). *Paradise of the Pacific: Approaching Hawai'i.* New York: Farrar, Straus and Giroux.

Morehead, Alan (1966). *The Fatal Impact: An Account of the Invasion of the South Pacific, 1767–1840.* London: Hamish Hamilton.

Morgan, Lewis Henry (1870). *Systems of Consanguinity and Affinity.* Washington, DC: Smithsonian Institution.

Morgan, Theodore (1948). *Hawai'i: A Century of Economic Change, 1778–1876.* Cambridge, MA: Harvard University Press.

Morgan, William M. (2011). *Pacific Gibraltar: U.S.-Japanese Rivalry and the Annexation of Hawai'i, 1885–1898.* Annapolis, MD: Naval Institute Press.

Moriyama, Alan Takeo (1985). *Imingaisha.* Honolulu: University of Hawai'i Press.

Mossakowski, Krysia N., and Turro S. Wongkaren (2016). "The Paradox of Discrimination, the 'Aloha Spirit,' and Symptoms of Depression in Hawai'i," *Hawai'i Journal of Medicine & Public Health,* 75 (1): 8–12.

Nakaso, Don (2008). "Should Hawai'i Rewrite Its Constitution – Again?," *Time,* October 30.

Nelligan, Peter J., and Harry V. Ball (1992). "Ethnic Juries in Hawai'i: 1865–1900," *Social Process in Hawai'i,* 34: 113–62.

Niebuhr, Reinhold (2015). *Reinhold Niebuhr: Major Works on Religion and Politics,* ed. Elisabeth Sifton. New York: Library of America.

Nordyke, Eleanor C. (1989). *Peopling of Hawai'i.* 2nd edn. Honolulu: University of Hawai'i Press.

Nunes, Shiho (1967). "The Hawai'i English Program: Brave New Venture," *Hawai'i Schools,* 4 (3): 14–17.

Okamura, Jonathan Y. (1994). "Why There Are No Asian Americans in Hawai'i: The Continuing Significance of Local Identity," *Social Process in Hawai'i,* 37: 131–78.

Pacific Commercial Advertiser (1864). November 6.

Pacific Commercial Advertiser (1891). "The Chinese Trouble at Kohala," *Pacific Commercial Advertiser,* September 7.

Pacific Commercial Advertiser (1897). "Japs Make Trouble: Eighty-One Unruly Laborers Are Locked up at Ewa," *Pacific Commercial Advertiser,* November 19.

Pacific Commercial Advertiser (1899a). "Cane Field Fire: Believed to Have Been Started by Fugitive Rioter," *Pacific Commercial Advertiser,* November 2.

Pacific Commercial Advertiser (1899b). " 'Jap' Proffer: Wanted to Assist Police to Subdue Chinese," *Pacific Commercial Advertiser,* November 3.

Pacific Commercial Advertiser (1899c). "The Pake Lost: Sympathy Strikers on Maui Are Defeated," *Pacific Commercial Advertiser,* January 10.

Park, Robert Ezra. (1928). "The Bases of Racial Prejudice," *Annals of the American Academy of Political and Social Science,* 140 (November): 11–20.

Park, Robert Ezra. (1938). "Introduction." In *An Island Economy: Ecological Succession in Hawai'i.* Eds. Andrew W. Lind, p. x–xvi. Honolulu: University of Hawai'i Press.

Pennybacker, Mindy (1991). "The Haole 'Rich Kids' School': An Update." In *Punahou: The History and Promise of a School of the Islands*, ed. Nelson Foster, pp. 119–49. Honolulu: Punahou School.

Perlin, John (2005). *A Forest Journey: The Role of Wood and Civilization*. Woodstock, VT: Countryman Press.

Plato (c.360BCE). *The Republic*. Buffalo, NY: Prometheus Books, 1986.

Pope Francis (2015). *Laudato Sí: On Care for Our Common Home*. Vatican: Vatican Press.

Porteus, Stanley D. (1962). *A Century of Social Thinking in Hawai'i*. Palo Alto, CA: Pacific Books.

Pukui, Mary Kawena (1986). "The Aloha Spirit Law." In *Barack Obama, the Aloha Zen President; How a Son of the 50th State May Revitalize America Based on 12 Multicultural Principles*, ed. Michael Haas, Appendix. Santa Barbara, CA: Praeger.

Ralston, Caroline (1978). *Grass Huts and Warehouses: Pacific Beach Communities of the Nineteenth Century*. Honolulu: University of Hawai'i Press.

Ramírez-Esparza, Nairán, Samuel D. Goslin, and James W. Pennebaker, "Paradise Lost: Unraveling the Puzzle of *Simpático*," *Journal of Cross-Cultural Psychology*, 39 (6): 703–15.

Rawls, John (1971). *A Theory of Justice*. Cambridge, MA: Harvard University Press.

Reinecke, John E. (1935). *Language and Dialect in Hawai'i*. M.A. thesis, Honolulu: University of Hawai'i.

Remnick, David (2010). *The Bridge: The Life and Rise of Barack Obama*. New York: Knopf.

Ross, Edward A. (1914). Old *World in the New: The Significance of Past and Present Immigration to the American People*. New York: Century.

Rousseau, Jean-Jacques (1762). *Of the Social Contract*. London: Penguin, 1968.

Russ, William A., Jr. (1959). *The Hawaiian Revolution*. Selinsgrove, PA: Susquehanna University Press.

Russ, William A., Jr. (1961). *The Hawaiian Republic*. Selinsgrove, PA: Susquehanna University Press.

Safire, William (1992). "On Language," *New York Times*, February 23.

Sahlins, Marshall D. (1958). *Social Stratification in Polynesia*. Seattle: University of Washington Press.

Schafer, Mark, and Stephen G. Walker, eds. (2006). *Beliefs and Leadership in World Politics: Methods and Applications of Operational Code Analysis*. New York: Palgrave Macmillan.

Schlesinger, Arthur M., Jr. (1991). *The Disuniting of America: Reflections on a Multicultural Society*. New York: Norton.

Schmitt, Robert C. (1965). "Demographic Correlates of Interracial Marriage in Hawai'i, 1848–1949," *Demography*, 2: 463–473.

Schmitt, Robert C. (1977). *Historical Statistics of Hawai'i*. Honolulu: University Press of Hawai'i.

Schmitt, Robert C., and Eleanor C. Nordyke (2001). "Death in Hawai'i: The Epidemics of 1848–1849," *Hawaiian Journal of History*, 35: 1–13.

Schneider, Louis, and Charles M. Bonjean, eds. (1973). *The Idea of Culture in the Social Sciences*. London: Cambridge University Press.

Sen, Amartya (1999). "Democracy as a Universal Value," *Journal of Democracy*, 10 (3): 3–17.

Sen, Amartya (2006). "The Uses and Abuses of Multiculturalism: Chili and Liberty," *New Republic*, February 27.

Shriver, Mark D. (2009). "Mixed Population Provides Insights into the Human Genetic Makeup," *ScienceDaily*, February 17. Accessed October 25, 2015.

Silva, Noenoe K. (2014). "Ke Kūʻē Kūpaʻa Loa Nei K/Mākua: A Memoir of 1898." In *A Nation Rising: Hawaiian Movements for Life, Land, and Sovereignty*, eds. Noelani Goodyear-Kaʻōpua, Ikaika Hussey, and Erin Kahunawaikaʻala Wright, Chapter 14. Durham, NC: Duke University Press.

Silver, Nate (2015). "Change Doesn't Usually Come This Fast," http://fivethirty eight/datalab, June 26. Accessed August 6, 2015.

Singer, Peter (2015). *The Most Good You Can Do: How Effective Altruism Is Changing Ideas About Living Ethically*. New Haven, CT: Yale University Press.

Smith, Adam (1776). *An Inquiry into the Nature and Causes of the Wealth of Nations*. New York: Modern Library, n.d.

Snow, Charles E. (1974). *Early Hawaiians*. Lexington, KY: University Press of Kentucky.

Spencer, Herbert (1855). *Principles of Psychology*. London: Longman, Brown, Green, Longmans.

Spooner, Lysander (c.1876). *The Lysander Spooner Reader*, ed. Jeffrey A. Tucker. San Francisco: Fox & Wilkes, 1992.

Sproat, D. Kapuaʻala (2010). "Water." In *The Value of Hawaiʻi: Knowing the Past, Shaping the Future*, eds. Craig Howes and Jon Osorio, pp. 187–94. Honolulu: University of Hawaiʻi Press.

Stannard, David E. (1989). *Before the Horror: The Population of Hawaiʻi on the Eve of Western Contact*. Honolulu: Social Science Research Institute, University of Hawaiʻi at Mānoa.

Stauffer, Robert H. (1983). "The Hawaiʻi-United States Treaty of 1826," *Hawaiian Journal of History*, 17: 55–8.

Stevens, Sylvester K. (1945). *American Expansion in Hawaiʻi, 1842–1898*. Harrisburg: Archives Publishing Company of Pennsylvania.

Stevenson, Robert Louis (1886). *The Strange Case of Dr. Jekyll and Mr. Hyde*. New York: Harper, 1997.

Stewart, C. S. (1970). *Journal of a Residence of the Sandwich Islands during the Years 1823–25*. Honolulu: University of Hawaiʻi Press.

Sullam, Brian (1976). *Bishop Estate: The Misused Trust*. Honolulu: Hawaiʻi Observer.

Takaki, Ronald T. (1983). *Pau Hana: Plantation Life and Labor in Hawaiʻi*. Honolulu: University of Hawaiʻi Press.

Taylor, Charles (1989). *Sources of the Self: The Making of Modern Identity*. Cambridge, MA: Harvard University Press.

Takaki, Ronald T. (2008). *A Different Mirror: A History of Multicultural America*. Rev. edn. Boston: Little, Brown.

Tobin, Richard J., and Dean Higuchi (1992). "Environmental Quality in America's Tropical Paradise." In *Politics and Public Policy in Hawaiʻi*, eds. Zachary A.

Smith and Richard C. Pratt, Chapter 7. Albany: State University of New York Press.

Truman, Harry S. (1950). "Letter to the President of the Senate on Statehood for Hawai'i and Alaska," November 27. Independence, MO: Harry S. Truman Library & Museum.

Tummons, Patricia (2010). "Terrestrial Ecosystems." In *The Value of Hawai'i: Knowing the Past, Shaping the Future*, eds. Craig Howes and Jon Osorio, pp. 163–9. Honolulu: University of Hawai'i Press.

Turner, Frederick Jackson (1893). "The Significance of the Frontier in American History," *Proceedings of the State Historical Society of Wisconsin*. Reprinted in Jackson, *The Frontier in American History*. Tucson: University of Arizona Press, 1896.

Tyler, Edward (1871). *Primitive Culture*. New York: Putnam's Sons, 1920.

U.S. Census (1902). *Twelfth Census of the United States, 1900; Population*. Washington, DC: Government Printing Office.

U.S. Census (1922). *Fourteenth Census of the United States, Taken in the Year 1920; Volume 3, Population: Composition and Characteristics of the Population by States*. Washington, DC: Government Printing Office.

U.S. Census (1962). *Census of Population, 1960; Characteristics of the Population: Hawai'i*. Washington, DC: Government Printing Office.

U.S. Census (1972). *1970 Census of Population; Detailed Characteristics: Hawai'i*. Washington, DC: Government Printing Office.

U.S. Census (1983). *1980 Census of Population: Characteristics of the Population; General Social and Economic Characteristics: Hawai'i*. Washington, DC: Government Printing Office.

U.S. Census (1993). *1990 Census of Population: Social and Economic Characteristics, Hawai'i*. Washington, DC: Government Printing Office.

U.S. Census (2000). *facfinder.census.gov.*

U.S. Departments of Interior and Justice (2000). *From Mauka to Makai: The River of Justice Must Flow Freely*. Washington, DC: Report on the Reconciliation Process between the Federal Government and Native Hawaiians.

Vives, Ruben (2015). "A Community of Cultures," *Los Angeles Times*, December 6.

Walker, Stephen G. (1990). "The Evolution of Operational Code Analysis," *Political Psychology*, 11: 403–18.

Widmer, Ted (2015). "Did the American Civil War Ever End?," *New York Times*, June 4.

Wikan, Unni (2002). *Generous Betrayal: Politics of Culture in the New Europe*. Chicago, IL: University of Chicago Press.

Wilcox, Bruce A., and Kepā Maly (2010). "Hawaiian Epidemics and Cultural Collapse: A Social-Ecological Perspective," www.hawaii.edu/publichealth/eco health/si/course-indighlth/-readings/WilcoxandMaly.pdf. Accessed June 4, 2014.

Wilkes, Charles (1845). *Narrative of the United States Exploring Expedition During the Years 1838, 1839, 1840, 1841, 1842*. London: Wiley and Putnam, 5 Volumes.

Wooden, Wayne S. (1981). *What Price Paradise: Changing Social Patterns in Hawai'i*. Washington, DC: University Press of America.

Zangwill, Israel (1909). *The Melting Pot: Drama in Four Acts*. New York: Macmillan.

Index